Out Of Body Ecstasy

Out Of Body Ecstasy

The Anywhere, Anytime, Orgasmic Experience

Allie Theiss

Also by Allie Theiss:

GYPSY MAGIC FOR THE LOVER'S SOUL

GYPSY MAGIC FOR THE PROSPERITY'S SOUL

GYPSY MAGIC FOR THE FAMILY'S SOUL

GYPSY MAGIC FOR THE DREAMERS'S SOUL

WELCOME TO THE NEIGHBORHOOD

All of the above titles are available in softcover & Kindle at Amazon.com

NOTE: The intent of the author is only to offer practices, techniques and formulas to help you in your quest for emotional, mental, spiritual, sexual, and physical empowerment. They should not be used as an alternative to professional medical, legal, mental, financial treatment and/or advice. Nor should it be used as an alternative to common sense. In the event you use any of the information in the book for yourself, which is your Divinely inspired right, the author and the publisher assume no responsibility for your actions.

ISBN-13 978-0-9771835-4-8
ISBN-10 0-9771835-4-8

Gypsy Girl Press does not participate in, endorse, or have any authority or responsibility concerning private business transactions between our authors and the public. All mail addressed to the author is forwarded but the publisher cannot, unless specifically instructed by the author, give out the author's address of phone number.

Gypsy Girl Press
PO Box 1511
Wooster, OH 44691

Dedication

To Bill this all started with you. I hope you are as happy, healthy, and peaceful in the physical reality as you are in the astral layers. Thank you for your energy and support. To Will, thank you for being my muse, and for supercharging — everything.

Table of Contents

Let's Talk Sex 15
And Then There Was Bill 18

CHAPTER ONE: The Basics 23

What is an Out of Body Experience? 24
What is Out of Body Ecstasy? 26
Is OBE Sex Considered Cheating? 28
White Light Protection 30
Preparing Your Inner Light 31
Preparing Your Energy 33

CHAPTER TWO: Preparing Your Space 37

A Sample Space 40
But Don't Take My Word For It 42
No Means No 43

CHAPTER THREE: The Energy Body 45

What Is The Energy Body? 46
Understanding Your Chakra's and Energy 49
Energy Signatures 50
Sharing Intimate Energy 54
Increasing Your Energy Fields 56

CHAPTER FOUR: Telepathic Sex 59

Has This Ever Happened To You? 60

Telepathic Connection 64
Telepathic Suggestion 72
But Don't Take My Word For It 74
Telepathic Foreplay 75
But Don't Take My Word For It 79
Telepathic Sex 81
But Don't Take My Word For It 91

CHAPTER FIVE: Dream Sex 93

Has This Ever Happened To You? 94
Dreamscape 97
Dream Portal 99
Dream Workstation 101
Dream Recall 103
Reality Check 104
Lucid Dreaming 105
But Don't Take My Word For It 108
Dream Foreplay 109
But Don't Take My Word For It 113
Dream Sex 114
But Don't Take My Word For It 123

CHAPTER SIX: Astral Sex 125

Has This Ever Happened To You? 126
Astral Travel 131
But Don't Take My Word for It 137
Astral Foreplay 138
But Don't Take My Word for It 142

Astral Sex 143
But Don't Take My Word for It 156

CHAPTER SEVEN: OBE Sex Protection.........157

CHAPTER EIGHT: OBE Sex Grids 167

CHAPTER NINE: OBE Sex Magic 175

What Is Magic 176
OBE Incenses 180
OBE Oils 185
OBE Sachets... 197
Metaphysical Aids 204

Appendix and Useful Bits 209

More About OBE 210
Useful Links 211
About Allie 2133

Let's Talk Sex

Is sex important? Sure it is! Not only is it important to keep a relationship alive and well, but also to beat away the blues, and boost immunity. According to WebMD (http://www.webmd.com/sex-relationships/guide/10-surprising-health-benefits-of-sex), having an active sex life can lead to:

1. Less stress, anxiety, and depression.
2. Low blood pressure.
3. A stronger immune system.
4. Better heart health.
5. Positive self-esteem.
6. Creates a deeper bond of intimacy.
7. Lowers pain.
8. Leads to peaceful sleep.
9. More ejaculations = less chance of prostate cancer.
10. Stronger pelvic floor muscles.
11. Encourages weight loss by burning calories.

All of the above sounds great, doesn't it? But life is busy, over scheduled, and stressful. Always being on the "go" makes having the time for sex at the bottom of our to-do list.

Unfortunately, as leading sexpert Dr. Pepper Swartz talks about in her *Whispers Media podcast*, "How To Be A Good Lover", if you don't use your sex drive you might as well give it a bus ticket and pack it a lunch - because it's heading out the door.

The sex drive is like any other important muscle or brain function. The more you use it, the more in tune and honed it is. You stop using it - it gets flabby - out of shape. When was the last time you saw a "couch potato" with a killer body? Probably never. Same principle applies to the sex drive. When you take time away from sex because of other commitments, a bad relationship, or exhaustion, your sex drive becomes lifeless.

But letting your sex drive get flabby isn't always a conscious decision. Some of the reasons your sex drive starts to wane include:

1. Depression/anxiety and their medications,
2. Heart disease, high blood pressure, cancer, diabetes, and their medications,
3. Over-the-counter cold/allergy medications,

4. Hormonal imbalance,
5. Trouble in the relationship - anger at your partner,
6. Smoking/alcohol/illegal drugs,
7. You're without a partner,

...and the list goes on.

Think about the last time your sex drive was in the basement. How did the rest of your life pan out? Did you notice that the other areas of your life fell apart? Like you were hitting a brick wall no matter what you tried?

If you look at Mike Dooley's "Leveraging the Universe" or Napoleon Hill's "Think and Grow Rich", your personal energy is crucial to how your life unfolds. Granted, both books talk about turning thoughts into energy (which is very true), but personal energy is personal energy no matter what.

Sexual energy/orgasmic release strengthen and increase a person's energy field. No sex and your energy body is depleted of its strength, thereby allowing negativity to eat away at the physical body, brain, and emotions. By working with your energy field and putting sex back on your "to-do" list, your energy increases, your stress decreases, and all else seems to fall into place.

Out of Body Ecstasy AKA OBE sex or OBE, uses your personal energy field to engage in sexual relations ranging from touching to sexual intercourse. OBE strengthens your energy field, adds passion to your relationships, and helps you find a new love or BFF with benefits.

Out of Body Ecstasy is a method of energy enhancement that can be done anywhere, anytime, with no special equipment needed.

And Then There Was Bill

It was late October 2002 my son was two years old and rarely took a nap. Heck, he rarely slept at night. To say I was running on fumes would be an understatement. During this time a neighbor suggested that I watch a movie. She and her family loved the movie and they all knew that I would love it too. What I would have loved is sleep, not a super long movie. However, the family was insistent that I watch it. After I put my son to bed for what I prayed would be an hour nap, I placed the movie into my VCR and hit play. The first thirty minutes I wanted to run screaming to the hills. Instead of turning it off, I went into the kitchen to make a grilled cheese sandwich.

I kept moving between the kitchen and the living room to see if I could find anything redeeming about this film. Then I saw a pair of the most gorgeous eyes flash across the screen. They looked vaguely familiar to me, but I had no idea WHY they would be familiar.

I grabbed my grilled cheese and ran back to the room so I could catch the face those eyes belonged to. When the actor appeared on screen, I thought he was attractive but I still had no clue to who he was. Fast forward a few scenes and my attractive actor was now against a group of bad guys. One by one he took them out.

He turned to look behind him at an approaching evil one and the look he had on his face…

HIT ME LIKE A TON OF BRICKS

My knees gave out and as I was falling to the ground, every single dream I've had my whole life where I only remembered the eyes – flashed before my face. But this time as the eyes popped up, the face filled out around them. Around the face the rest of the dream filled in around him. By the time I landed on my back, I had flipped through hundreds, maybe thousands, of dreams.

The next thing I know I open my eyes to have two dogs and four cats staring at me. Indiana Jones, a beagle-dachshund mix, nudged my head with his nose to see if I was OK. I didn't know what I was, except not dead.

After I removed six animals from my body and sat up on the couch, I thought to myself, "What the hell was that?"

That, my dear friends, was Bill. A man who forever changed the course of my life when he opened my eyes up to the possibilities of which I cannot see with my human eyes. Because of him I now overflow with love from twin flames, soul mates, soul clusters, the discovery of my entire soul group, and development of Out of Body Ecstasy.

Note: About the men I'll talk about in this book. Bill, Ted, Will, and Vincent are very much alive, and yes, are real people. I have met Bill and Will. Both encounters were life-changing. Ted and Vincent are just a matter of Divine timing.

CHAPTER ONE:
The Basics

What is an Out of Body Experience?

Out of body experiences are short-term episodes where the conscious mind, via the energy body, separates from the physical body enabling a person to engage in and observe the world from outside their physical perspective. An out of body experience is just as vivid and real as a physical experience.

The energy body represents a key component in an out of body experience, as not only is it the vehicle of exploration and sexual stimulation, but it is also the consciousness in charge of regeneration and repair of our body and energy anatomy. The energy body interfaces between the conscious and the unconscious mind with seven distinctive energy fields making up the entire energy body.

There are three different methods to launch an out of body experience:

a. Telepathy – Have you ever "heard" the thoughts of another? Alternatively, had a non-verbal talk with a spouse or best friend? Telepathy is the energetic transfer of touch, ideas, thoughts, emotions, feelings, and sound. A telepathic connection is a bond with the mental energy body that connects two or more minds into the same energetic wavelength to utilize telepathy.

b. Dream – When was the last time you woke up from a dream and remembered vivid details? With dream travel/visits, you are asleep with your astral energy body separating from your physical body and taking off into the dreamscape. When the dream recall is so vivid that it appeared real, you shared a visit with another person while he or she was sleeping.

c. Astral – Did you ever have an experience where it felt like you "fell" onto your bed? That was your energy body returning from astral travel. Astral travel occurs when your astral energy body separates from your physical body. This separation is Astral Projection. With astral travel, as with dreaming, there is no limit to what you can do, become, or travel to.

When you interact with another energy, via one of the three methods, you are also exchanging energy. Some of your energy transfers to them as some of their energy transfers to you. Be careful to whom you choose to connect. If you connect to a less than scrupulous person, his or her energy will become a part of who you are until you do an energy cleansing.

What is Out of Body Ecstasy?

Out of Body Ecstasy sex is a form of energy enhancement, sexual play, and sexual satisfaction that involves the use of your mind, your energy fields, and your senses. No physical parts merge, touch or copulate in any manner during an OBE sex experience.

Your mind in conjunction with the astral energy field can make a telepathic connection to another human (telepathic sex), your astral energy body separates from your physical body during REM (dream sex) or your astral energy body can separate from your physical body while you are awake and conscious (astral sex).

Whether or not you are in a relationship or single, OBE can enhance your physical sex life by providing your senses with the stimuli needed to cause arousal and even orgasmic release.

During OBE your physical body can feel the touch of your sexual partner, can smell their scent, hear their voice, and taste their body. How can this help to enhance your sex life? It's a known fact that healthy sex lives translates into a healthier, happier physical existence as it works to lower blood pressure, lose weight and is a good workout for your heart -- not to mention that it energizes your energy fields to attract good things to you.

OBE turns you on and tunes you into your sexuality. Upon waking from your vivid dream, returning from an astral visit or coming out of your day dream, if you have a partner they can enjoy the benefits of your exploration. If you do not have a partner, you will benefit from exploring your own body. If you did not have an orgasm during the OBE, your physical body will be so turned on that you will have to **DO SOMETHING** to experience a sexual release.

It is important to note here that when you are engaged in OBE sex that "sex" does not have to occur. You can merge your energy fields and simply enjoy one another by desiring, loving, and energizing. It's your energy and you can do whatever you wish to do with it. No two people experience something the same way and this includes OBE sex.

Out of body ecstasy can be experienced by old and young alike: couples, singles, and the disabled or physically impaired.

Is OBE Sex Considered Cheating?

This question comes up a lot from people in loveless or sexless relationships. If he or she strays outside the relationship with OBE sex, would it be considered cheating? Cheating is all in the eyes of the partner.

OBE sex involves pure energy and no physical parts merge. Each person views what is cheating differently. To some it is sharing personal information, to others it is a kiss, and still others sexual intercourse or oral sex. If you are in a sexless relationship, OBE sex can help spice up your physical sex life with your partner as the intensity of the OBE encounters will turn your body on so much that you will want to find release with your physical partner. In a healthy relationship, OBE sex isn't *replacement* sex – it is *additive* sex (meaning it ADDS to a relationship). In a loveless relationship OBE sex can help reignite forgotten feelings towards one another.

OBE sex is different from online & phone sex because with online/phone sex people usually do it so that they do not have to have sex with their partner. Two people on two separate ends of a computer/phone are getting each off so that they each can achieve a physical orgasm.

Each person who was engaged in the computer/phone sex then does not wish to have sex with their partner. This is only meant as my point of view. Each individual must come to their own conclusion.

White Light Protection

OBE protection is covered more extensively at the end of this book. No, there is no need for birth control during OBE sex. I'm not talking about that kind of protection! What you need is to protect yourself from lower energies zapping your strength and hanging on for all it's worth.

To keep yourself protected during an OBE experience, surround yourself in a brilliant white light. It's easy to do. Just close your eyes and imagine the sky opening up and surrounding you in a bright white light. Hold the image for a few seconds, then be on your way.

Preparing Your Inner Light

Before starting on the path to OBE experiences, I think it's a good idea to prepare or strengthen your inner light. The inner light is of course our soul. The reason it needs strengthened is that although at birth it shines nice and bright, throughout our lives we shovel a lot of crap on top of our soul. Stuff like, "I'll be alone for the rest of my life," "I'm fat," or "I'll not amount to anything."

With every derogatory statement, our inner light gets muddied up. Making it more difficult to shine through the self-imposed crap pile.

When your light is dim, you will attract lower energies during your OBE experiences. In an upcoming section I talk about sharing intimate energy. When you have sex with someone, whether it be OBE sex or physical sex, your energies co-mingle. That is why it is important that you keep your energy vibration high and strong so that you only attract to you higher vibrational souls/people.

Techniques to Prepare Your Inner Light

1. Get rid of self-sabotaging thoughts and beliefs. Call in guides, angels, or whomever or whatever Divine energy you wish to invoke to take away your negative beliefs. Say in a loud commanding voice, "Take these negative thoughts and beliefs. I AM DONE with them!" I find it helpful to imagine a shovel digging out my throat, heart & solar plexus chakras to release a black goo into the Universe.

2. Consciously be aware of your thoughts. When a negative, self-limiting thought pops in, push it out of your mind and bring in a positive thought.

3. Think about what makes you happy. More important - FEEL the happiness associated with the thought.

4. White light isn't only for protection. Imagine the white light originating from INSIDE your body, radiating outward. Your physical body is the middle of a white-light sun. This uplifts your energy from the inside out!

Preparing Your Energy

It is a good idea to prepare your physical & energy bodies for OBE sex just as it is important to prepare your OBE space. If you are having trouble making an OBE sex connection or simply want to connect easier, consider utilizing one or more of the below tips.

- Take a bath or shower. Disposing of the physical filth picked up during the day and washing it away will help you perform better and develop better concentration. When you feel clean, the energy around you does, as well.

- Refrain from drinking alcohol, or taking drugs (illegal and/or prescription) at least six hours prior to OBE. Drugs and alcohol do not add to the experience. Yes, they relax you. However, they also blur the lines between hallucinations/reality and make it difficult for you to remember the experience.

- Make sure that you are not hungry or thirsty, as feeling either can take your focus away from the task at hand.
- Do not eat red meat at least twelve hours prior to OBE. Red meat grounds your energy. Makes it more difficult to achieve OBE.
- Do eat a diet rich in organic fruits & vegetables.
- Consider taking at least one of these three herbs for increasing focus, memory, and brain power (wise to consult with your doctor prior to starting any of these herbs):
    - **Rhodiola Rosea**- fuels sexual energy, cuts down on stress, enhances mood, helps with sleep, fights fatigue, improves memory, increases alertness, mental focus, and boosts attention span.
    - **Bacopa Monnieri** - boosts your memory, helps calm anxiety and depression, supports cognitive and focus issues, plus lessens memory loss.
    - **Ginkgo Biloba** - it increases blood flow to

the legs, ears, eyes and brain, which helps enhance the memory. Plus for those on depression or anxiety medication, ginkgo biloba can help with the libido issues caused by those drugs.

- Stay away from GMO (Genetically Modified Organism) products. This can be a daunting task as most commercial foods you buy are produced with GMO altered grains. GMO's not only ground your energy making it difficult to achieve OBE, they make you unhealthy. To see a list of companies to avoid at the grocery store, go here.
- Wear comfortable clothes.
- Meditate or day dream for at least 10 minutes before you begin. This helps to calm your mind and push out the clutter of daily thoughts that could interfere with the energy process.

CHAPTER TWO:
Preparing Your Space

Where you engage in OBE sex is as important as the techniques used to have OBE experiences. Would you work in your office without a desk and computer? Probably not. Same rule of thought applies to OBE. You want to find a place where you will not be disturbed. This is especially important for dream and astral sex. Once out of the dream or astral state, it is difficult to slip right back in and return to the exact location and pick up at the precise moment you left.

Your space affects not only your OBE experiences, but your physical life. You should make sure that:

- The space is quiet where you will not be disturbed.
- The room is comfortable with either a comfortable bed, chair/couch, or floor mat/pillows.
- The walls should have a cool color such as blue, purple, or green.
- Red is an aggressive color as well as a passionate one. Red is good as a secondary color on accessory items, such as lamps, pictures, or stones.
- Orange is a sexual, creative color and used in OBE sex. It is a great color to have in the bedroom if that is your OBE space. However, if you are using an office or another part of your

home as OBE central, keep orange to the accessories in the room.

- Yellow is a communicative, confidence color. Great color if you are using an office or a secondary room for your OBE space. However, if you are using your bedroom, keep yellow to the accessories in your room.
- A secure place for incense to burn or an essential oil diffuser.
- The space is clutter-free.
- The area is organized.
- No electronic devices are in the room. This includes TV, computer, and cell phone. The electronic waves that emit from the devices interfere with OBE experiences. If the room has to have them in it, say in an office or living room, make sure they are off and unplugged prior to trying OBE.

A Sample Space

A client came to me and was just beside himself because he could not get an OBE sex experience to take place. So I asked him, what does your space look like? He replied…

"I use my spare bedroom for my OBE experiences. It has beige walls with a few pictures hanging on it. The bed has a blue comforter and there are two brown dressers, one with a mirror. Most of the floor is stacked with boxes from my parent's house. They died several years ago."

I asked him how often does he vacuum the floor and take a dust cloth to the dressers. He admitted that it has been five years since he's done anything like that in that room - same time the boxes moved in. A dusty, cluttered room just will not have the energy flow he needs for OBE. My advice for him was to either to conduct OBE sex in another room, or get this room into shape. He chose to stay in that room.

The changes I proposed included:

- Moving the boxes out of the room into either the basement/attic or renting storage.
- Clean the room by dusting, vacuuming, and removing spider webs/dead bugs.
- Paint the walls a soothing sky blue. Relaxes him so that it is easier to slip into an OBE state.

- Add an orange or burnt orange shade comforter to the bed for sexual energy.
- A few red accessories such as a candle and picture frames with pictures of happy moments for passion.
- Paint the dressers either green (for love) or white (communication to guides/angels).

My client followed my advice. When he attempted OBE sex afterwards, at first it was dicey as he was still hesitant that it would work. But after time and practice, he was able to enjoy OBE sex. He uses the room so much for his OBE activities, that he is considering making it his main bedroom! If so, I think he'll notice an increase in his OBE/physical sex activities!

But Don't Take My Word For It

Choose a place where you want to experience OBE sex. Take a look around the space. Is it clean? Non-cluttered? What colors are dominant in the room?

Action Steps

1. Dust and vacuum
2. Put away the clutter
3. Look back to the beginning of this section and determine what color changes should be made.

No Means No

One last little tid bit before jumping into the energy body. Treat the OBE world as you would the physical world. When someone says, "No," respect it and move on. If you feel resistance to your telepathic connection/sex request. That is a NO. Move on. Someone kicks you out of a dream or disappears from your sight in the astral layers that is a NO. Move on.

To ignore a NO amounts to rape. What happens to the energy body affects the physical body, the emotions, and thoughts. Although it is not physical rape, it will leave scars and incur pain. The fallout will linger.

NO MEANS NO!

CHAPTER THREE:
The Energy Body

What Is The Energy Body?

Energy is more than the fuel that lets you flip a switch and "poof" a light turns on. Energy is all around us. It is the lamp, the light, your dog, radio stations, trees, plants, you - through you and around you. In fact, there is no place energy does not exist.

In other words, energy is everything
and everything is energy.

In a book called, *E-Squared*, author Pam Grout wrote that according to quantum physics, the invisible energy realm is the primary governing force of the material realm. So in other-words, what happens in energy duplicates itself materially. I would agree with that 100%. That's what makes Out of Body Ecstasy work.

Because energy works within and around you, fields of energy surround your physical body and work for the betterment of you and only you. Each person's energy fields are unique, but they all follow the same format.

The belief among those who experience OBE and/or who do energy healing is that humans have three major energy planes and seven major energy fields that make up a person's energy body.

a. Spiritual Plane – the outer most energy field.

   i. Archetypal - the energy field contains our soul's copy of our Akashic Records: what we have done, we are we have been and the current map of our destiny in this lifetime.

   ii. Spiritual - the energy field reflects our boundless energy into our psychological, social, and physical realities.

   iii. Mental - the energy field builds our relationship to our Destiny Markers, past and present karma/karmic connections, and inner life.

b. Astral Plane – the middle energy field.

   iv. We create and experience our astral and dream out of body experiences through this medium. This energy field is the component to look within and to develop our creative side. Intention, positive self-image, visual learning, visualization and healing, manifestation, and success generate and reflect in this energy level.

c. Physical Plane – the energy field closest to the physical body.

   v. Emotional - the energy field carries the luggage of

our feelings and emotional projection and response. We experience our telepathic connection through here.

vi. Etheric – the energy field is a blueprint or energy archetype for the physical body. It creates and maintains the body form. We experience telepathic sex experiences from here.

vii. Physical - the energy field reflects physical trauma, cell memory, physical health, and physiological beliefs and emotions.

Learning about energy and our energy bodies is complex. There is much more to energy than what I wrote here. I encourage you to explore on your own. It's a fascinating subject!

Some of my favorite books on energy are:

Energy Medicine by Donna Eden

Vibrational Energy by Richard Gerber, M.D

Energy Work by Robert Bruce

Frequency: The Power of Personal Vibration by Penney Peirce

Understanding Your Chakra's and Energy Colors

Energy portals or chakras keep our energy body and therefore our physical body in tiptop shape. The chakras connect via a chakra highway. If there is a blockage in one chakra, it causes an energy jam along the chakra route. Think of it like traveling down any road in Los Angeles – if there is an accident or delay – your odds of getting to your destination in time has crawled to a stop bringing with it frustration, anxiety and stress. It applies to chakras and their energy route. To deal with a blockage one must understand each of the main chakras and their corresponding color.

There are seven main chakras and energy colors:

- **Base or Root Chakra**: Red – passion, security, and aggression.
- **Sacral Chakra**: Orange – creativity, well-being, and sexual energy.
- **Solar Plexus Chakra**: Yellow – confidence, personal power, and attraction.
- **Heart Chakra**: Green/pink – unity, peace, and love.
- **Throat Chakra**: Blue – communication, will, and integrity.
- **Third Eye Chakra**: Violet – intuition, imagination, and knowledge.
- **Crown Chakra**: Indigo – oneness, serenity, and beauty.

Energy Signatures

During an OBE experience – whether it is for sex or just to travel/connect – it's our energy bodies that are doing the OBE. Because of this we are able to shift our appearance from what we look like in our human bodies to anything we want. We can be a male or female (as we've been both in past lives) we can be any race we choose (again in every life we will each get to live in a different race – some more than once).

But even though we can change our physical or energy appearance – there are two things we cannot alter and that follows us not only in the OBE world, but from lifetime to lifetime:

Our Eyes

The shape may change – the size – but never the color or the glint of our eyes when someone looks into them. Since each of our souls are unique – we each have a unique glint. Our eyes truly are the windows to the soul.

When I first realized that Bill was a significant soul in my existence, the realization hit me when I looked into his eyes. His eyes took me back through our past lives into the present. In each of our lives, he looked different, but he eyes were the same. That is how I first recognized him. As I learn about energy, I discovered…

Our Energy Signatures

We each carry a different energy print – much like a fingerprint – no two are alike.

One night as I fell asleep I was in the need for some dream sex - so I went off in search of Vincent_for some steamy lovin`. He'd been around me all day long, so I knew that he shouldn't be hard to find. I entered into a dream and landed in a burnt out building - if felt like a house in France during WW2.

I turned and there he was -- just leaning against a wall staring at me. I smiled -- but something inside me was saying this was off, something wasn't right.

He commented that he liked what I had done to my hair. In a few short steps, he was in front of me, kissing me gently on the lips. Although the kiss felt good - it didn't feel right. I didn't get that same surge of energy that I normally did. This got me to thinking - who was this guy?

I put my arms around him and hugged him tight (normally I would have had an allover energy surge - but now, nadda), pulled back and looked into his eyes. His eyes were brown, but didn't hold the same spark as the norm. I asked how he'd been he said he was fine --- with that he started kissing my neck, his hand fondled my breast. I gave him a little push and took a step back.

I looked him dead in the eyes and asked who he was -- he of course said Vincent. But I knew damn well this wasn't him. And that's what I said with the adage - try again. He's like, come on babe and took a step towards me. I threw up a thick protection wall and told him to stay back.

His appearance morphed into someone else - someone I don't know in the physical sense, but was vaguely familiar (like from a past life). He asked how I knew. I told him, his energy signature is off, it's not Vincent's. He said that it was easy to track me down because my energy is so high because I practice OBE and he knew what Vincent actually looked like - but that he was hoping he could have gotten further with me before I figured it out - he missed the feel of my skin. As he said I'll be seeing you again - Vincent did come out of right field and plowed right into him - grabbed him by the neck and told him to stay away. Then he threw him through the wall -and I mean through like the wall was liquid - the wall didn't look damaged.

Because I could sense Vincent's energy signature (that energy surge was present); I lowered my wall and allowed him to come near me. This was a fine example of just that - this person looked like Vincent, sounded like Vincent -- but energetically it didn't feel like Vincent.

If you ever encounter such a problem while you're dreaming (and if you do engage in dream sex, your energy will expand making it easier for all sorts of people to find you), imagine a thick white wall of energy coming out of the ground and moving upwards, closing above you. Then think of another place you would rather be and you should go there. If this person follows you, you can ask your angels and guides to come in for projection. All you have to do is call them with something like this: "Guardian Angels and Spirit Guides surround me with your protection and keep me safe from harm. Thank you". OBE Sex protection isn't about safe sex, but it is about safety.

I do know that I will be on the look out for this guy now with this energy signature.

Sharing Intimate Energy

Paying attention to whom you share your sexual energy with is one of the most important things you can do. Having sexual relations with another, whether it is in the physical sense or via OBE, intertwines your energy body (all seven layers) with the energy body of the other person. No matter how insignificant the sexual experience was (a quick kiss, one night stand, or a brief affair) it still leaves behind a little bit of them. This "leave behind" energy affects your energy field, therefore your mind, emotions, and surrounding world.

Never have sex (physical or OBE) with a person/soul/energy you wouldn't want in your life forever.

When you have sex with anyone you merge with their energy. It doesn't matter if it is OBE sex, physical (vaginal/anal) sex, or oral sex — anytime you are intimate with another person (or people) you absorb their energy and they absorb your energy.

If you have sex with positive, loving, uplifting people – that wonderful energy is absorbed and uplifts you. If you have sex with negative, pessimistic, unstable, depressive people – that energy may very well have you crashing down and uninterested in day to day life.

Keep in mind that if this person sleeps with a variety of people, they absorb their energy. A married man or woman has absorbed their spouses' energy and will mix it with your energy if you are the other man or woman and vice versa.

So the next time you jump into bed with someone or want to hook up for OBE sex – keep in mind that unless they cleanse their energy on a regular basis, you will be getting intimate with whomever they have been intimate with. Make sure you connect with positive uplifting souls!

Increasing Your Energy Fields

The energy bodies respond better to OBE travel and sex if you "rev up" your energy bodies prior to your OBE attempts.

When a person has no energy, there is a block or blocks in the chakra highway. Without the energy flowing, as it should, OBE is very difficult to accomplish. The best solution is to stimulate the chakras to restart the energy flow and therefore strengthen the energy body.

Most people do not both with the second level of chakras on the hands and feet. That is where we're going to start.

I originally learned the paintbrush technique from energy master Robert Bruce. I took the basics from him and adapted it.

Did you ever watch the original "The Karate Kid" with Ralph Macchio (Daniel) and Pat Morita (Mr. Miyagi)? There is a famous scene where Mr. Miyagi is making Daniel paint a fence. With the paintbrush in hand, Daniel must keep his wrist limp as he slowly draws the paintbrush upwards and downward on each fence board.

In case you do not know the scene referenced, watch it on YouTube: http://youtu.be/R37pbIySnjg

Paintbrush Energy Exercise

Now that you have that image in your mind, rest your left elbow on a hard surface with your arm up, palm open, and fingers pointing towards the sky. This is the “fence board.” Use the fingertips of your right hand as the “paintbrush,” to “paint” repeatedly your left hand from wrist to fingertips. Close your eyes. Pay attention to HOW the painting motion feels on your palm and wrist. FEEL it rather than SEE it. Continue doing this for 30 seconds, while being in the moment.

After the 30 seconds stop physically painting and instead mentally paint. Move the energy up and down your hand and wrist with your mind. FEEL the energy move. Keep doing this and you will start to feel different sensations like tingling, pressure, tickling, and vibrations. Feeling any of these sensations means, you have successfully stimulated your secondary chakras in your hand.

Switch hands and repeat.

Repeat this same exercise with the soles of each foot, using your foot as the fence board and your fingertips as the paintbrush.

Ready to be supercharged? Try the exercise below.

Main Chakras Exercise

1. Using the paintbrush technique you learned above, you're going to use it on each of the major chakras.

2. It is up to you on if you start with the base chakra and work up to the crown chakra, or from the crown chakra to the base chakra. But it has to be one end or the other.

3. For example, I will start with the base chakra and work up.

4. Close your eyes and locate your base chakra. With your fingertips, "paint" your chakra red. Imagine red energy streaming from your fingertips into your chakra. After 30 seconds, stop using your fingertips and allow the red energy to paint the chakra. Remember, it is important to FEEL the energy more than it is to SEE it. Do this for as long as you want, waking up the chakra with tingling, vibrations, etc…

5. Move up to your sacral chakra and repeat step 4 with orange energy.

6. Move up to your solar plexus chakra and repeat step 4 with yellow energy.

7. Move up to your heart chakra and repeat step 4 with green or pink energy.

8. Move up to your throat chakra and repeat step 4 with blue energy.

9. Move up to your third-eye chakra and repeat step 4 with violet energy.

10. Move up to your crown chakra and repeat step 4 with indigo energy.

This is a great exercise to do whenever you feel stuck in life as it unclogs the chakra highway!

CHAPTER FOUR:
Telepathic Sex

Has This Ever Happened To You?

"Lisa and Ben"

Lisa sat at work like any other day typing away at her computer keyboard when all of a sudden she felt horny. Her thoughts immediately went to Ben. But she wasn't thinking of Ben before she got turned on, so why did she get sexually aroused and think of Ben? She tried to logically think it through and wasn't coming up with answer. So she pushed him and her horniness from her mind and continued on with her work.

About an hour later she was talking with a co-worker at the vending machine when she felt her left nipple tingle. She loved it when Ben teased her nipples with his mouth, so her thoughts went immediately to him. Flustered, she excused herself from the co-worker and went into the one-person restroom. Leaning on the bathroom sink, she could feel a tingling on her neck. If she wasn't looking in the mirror, she would have sworn that he was behind her.

The sensations continued to her lips, her breasts, down to the dampness between her legs. Inside her head her voice screamed, "This is nuts — get back to work," but she didn't want it to stop. It felt so good — so Ben-like. God she missed him. Ben was halfway around the world in the UK for business while she was home in Chicago.

They had nightly Skype video chats, but it was never enough. She longed to feel him inside of her. What was happening right now felt like he was thrusting inside of her. Lisa couldn't take it any longer. Masturbating to the sensation of Ben thrusting in and out of her, Lisa rode the sensations to orgasmic release.

Later that evening, during the nightly Skype chat, Ben asked Lisa if she felt anything sexual today towards him. Surprised by his question, she hesitantly answered yes - then added, but why did he ask? Ben admitted that after work he went back to his flat and couldn't stop thinking about her. The more he thought of her, the hornier he became. So he closed his eyes and imagined that he was there with her at work having his way with her! But then he got a phone call and had to run out for work. When he came back an hour later he resumed thinking about throwing her on her boss's desk and ramming into her until she came all over him. Lisa told Ben what had happened to her at work and that she couldn't leave the bathroom until she had taken care of herself!

That was when Lisa Googled "telepathic sex" and found yours truly. Since that point in time, I worked with the couple and now they can slip into telepathic sex with one another all the time - no matter if Ben is out of the country or just down the street.

It has taken their relationship to a new, energetically and spiritually, deeper level. Before Lisa and Ben could master "on the fly" telepathic sex, they had to master a telepathic connection.

"Samantha"

Samantha had been blissfully single for the last three years. With her marriage ending up in flames and working 60+ hrs. a week to make up for the layoffs, sex was the last thing on her mind. One night she was halfway comatose in front of her TV watching some program she could've cared less about. Suddenly, she felt a twinge of sexual excitement between her legs. That area has been "dead" for years, so she thought she was imagining it. But it came again, this time stronger than the first time. She tried to pay attention to the TV show. However, the more she tried not to pay attention to her sexual excitement, the stronger it became. Finally, she turned off the TV and went to bed. She tossed and turned for hours, trying to ignore the tingles on her nipples, the pressure on her lips, and the increasing wetness between her legs. She couldn't take it anymore and masturbated herself into an orgasmic release. Happy and exhausted, she fell asleep.

The next evening it was a repeat of the previous night. Except this time she didn't try to fight it. Instead she flowed with the sexual excitement. After her orgasm, she stayed awake for a while, thinking about why this is happening. What is going on? Is she imagining it? What would her friends think if she told them?

She felt comfortable with the energy as if she knew that the energy was a person she already knew. But how was that possible? None of it made sense to her. Based on her academic background in IT, she could not logically figure out what was going on. That is when she searched the Internet for an explanation and found me. We had a few sessions together and it was discovered that the energy belonged to a man in her soul group. He found her by reaching out to the Universe and putting it out there that he was looking for people in his soul group of the opposite sex. Her energy was the one that connected and responded. Although the two have yet to meet in person, they still connect via a telepathic connection/sex several times a week!

Telepathic Connection

Telepathy is the energetic transfer of touch, ideas, thoughts, emotions, feelings, and sound. A Telepathic Connection is the energy bond that connects two or more minds into the same energetic wavelength to utilize telepathy.

Communication between people without a word spoken is a talent that spans centuries. Our mind, like radio or TV towers, emits and steadily receives electrical energies. We cannot see this happening, but we know that it happens as when we flip on a TV or radio our program "magically" appears it seems, out of thin air!

Our minds work exactly the same way. We broadcast emotions, moods, thoughts, attitudes, fragments of our personality, unknowingly every day. Everything that emits energy also absorbs energy. Meaning, that with practice we can learn to read and speak to one another without ever moving our mouths!

A stranger cannot listen in on your private thoughts - nor can you act like a psychic spy and barrel in to retrieve another person's thoughts. We all have a natural force field, or barrier that protects our thoughts from others. We do not have to think about it for it to be there as it is as automatic as a sunrise.

However, we can give people permission to read our minds by mentally lowering this field by simply telling ourselves to do so.

Types of Telepathic Connections

There are two ways to have a telepathic connection: Dominant and Non-Dominant

Dominant – You are in control of the connection and decide what to talk about and/or what activity to engage in. *For example - if I connected to Ted and sent him the thoughts and took control of the sexual experience.*

Non-Dominant – You are passive in the connection and let the dominant person decide what will or what will not happen in the connection. If you want to get to know someone better – this is the way to go as you can observe what motivates them. *For example - Will connecting to me and controlling the conversation and the sexual experience.*

Types of Thoughts

Everyone has different layers of thoughts. From those thoughts which are easily accessible, to those thoughts that wish to remain secret.

Public Thoughts

These thoughts sit close to the surface and are easily accessible. They usually contain what has happened during the day and/or what you are presently working on when the connection happens. *Example: take the dog out, do homework, call mom, pick up wife's dry cleaning.*

Private Thoughts

These are normally public thoughts that you want to keep out of the "public eye" so you shield them to make it harder for someone to tap into these thoughts. A way to make thoughts private is not to say (in your mind or out loud) what you are thinking. If you see someone attractive – don't say to yourself mentally that the person is attractive. When you do not mentally say what you are thinking – then it is not as easy to access those thoughts. *Example: Me seeing Ted and thinking, "Hot damn I'd like to eat him!" If he connected to me, he "hear" those thoughts without a lot of effort.*

Inner Thoughts

These are thoughts that are hard to get to unless you are very strong telepathically.

These inner thoughts are a combination of your pasts, the present, and your wishful future. Thoughts are combined with daydreams and memories; emotions, fears, feelings, sounds and pictures.

Thoughts and memories relate by similarity – with practice, you will be able to tell the difference between the two.

Connecting

Everything is energy and energy is everything. Following that stream of thought, Ben and Lisa were already connected. However, it was not a conscious connection. They did not know they were doing telepathic sex until they found me and I told them what it was. Because it was not a conscious connection, neither of them could know that the connection was there until they talked to one another about their day. By connecting telepathically both Lisa and Ben will consciously know of the connection and thereby feel more connected.

How to Make a Telepathic Connection

1. Relax, sit comfortably, and close your eyes.

2. Shift your focus upward, above your ears, and sense the temporal lobe sections.

3. Focus in on a person you wish to communicate with.

    a. If there is no specific person you wish to connect to, imagine the qualities in the person you want to connect to. Example - nice, wealthy, studious. If you want to include the physical attributes to make it easier for you - that's ok. Try not to get hung up though, on the outer facade.

4. Imagine a white light emitting from your temporal lobes, wrapping around the target person's head. If this is difficult to do, instead imagine a white light emitting from your whole body and that whole white light engulfs the target person so that you two are in a big white light bubble.

5. You will know if you connect telepathically if you feel pressure, vibrations, tingling, or tickling any place on your body – but in particular either in your solar plexus or throat chakra.

6. Be open to whatever you experience. Do not try too hard - do not force your concentration.

7. Feel how a multitude of impressions/words/sounds seems to pour into your mind through the temporal lobes.

8. Notice the sensation of heightened attunement that opens up in your solar plexus/throat -- FEEL the communications.

9. Allow your remaining senses to come into the equation.

10. Strengthen the connection. You may feel a bit light-headed and/or your stomach may do some flip-flops – this is normal.

11. Mentally send a message. At first, make it short like, "Hi" or "I love you."

12. Listen for a reply.
13. Continue the conversation for as long as you can hold your attention on that person.
14. When you are finished, imagine the white light coming loose from the person's head or body and draw it back into your temporal lobes. Sometimes it helps to imagine double doors shutting once you bring the white light back to you.
15. Note your impressions. I like to write them in a journal and keep track.

Allie's Example

I'm sitting in the back of a college classroom of 150+ students. I'm bored out of my mind. So I decide to connect to Will. I lean back, close my eyes, and concentrate on the space right above my ear lobes. Feels a bit tingly when I do that!

I think about Will; his dirty blond hair pulled back in a ponytail, scruffy facial hair, old & dirty green army jacket & pants, big ole black boots. He has a cocky grin, beautiful blue eyes. Once I have his image in my mind, I concentrate above my ear lobes and send out energy "beams" to Will, wrapping the light around his head.

(If it wasn't Will and I was just trying to connect to not anyone specific, I would think about a nice, southern man, with the energy of a teenager and the patience of an older man. A creative soul with striking blue eyes.)

I give the connection about 10 - 20 sec before I start to feel "funny" in my solar plexus chakra and get lightheaded. I hear "Missed you." I can see and feel him kiss me on the right cheek.

I send more light along our connection and turn the white light a bit yellowish. My stomach feels like I'm on a roller coaster. I hate that feeling. Makes me ill.

With the connection strengthened, I send back "Missed you too."

He replied, "Alright then."

I can hear the person next to me talking to the person next to her. It's distracting. Not being able to hold the connection for much longer, I pull back the light and close the connection.

I opened my eyes and jotted down a few notes from the exchange to transfer to my journal later that night.

Telepathy needs to be conducted with honesty, integrity and compassion for the other person's thoughts, feelings, and emotions. There is always a chance that you could learn personal information – and unless you have this person's permission, you will need to keep what is private - private. If you betray their trust, future connections will be more difficult as their natural force field will be blocking the connection.

The target person does not always consciously know that you are connecting, but will still respond subconsciously. Even if the connection is subconscious on their end, your connection with them will strengthen.

Now for those of you who are single and are looking to connect to a twin flame, soul mate, or a potential boyfriend/girlfriend. You will not be able to connect to anyone you do not know. This knowing can be here in the present, from a past life, or in a future life. Your soul, his or her soul, will know if you two KNOW one another. Only then can the connection occur. If you do not know them (think celebrities) nor will you, there will not be a connection.

You cannot force the connection – I cannot stress that point enough. If you meet resistance, that means no. And a no is a no in the energy world just like a no is a no in the physical world.

Telepathic Suggestion

You can use a telepathic connection to not only receive, but also to suggest. Suggestions get easier to make and have the other person receive the stronger you are telepathically. Keep in mind that suggestions are just that – a suggestion – they are not a command of any kind. They are quick, to the point and usually do not last longer than a flash.

You cannot telepathically suggest to someone something that would be out of the person's comfort zone. They can be used to suggest simple things like; "Rub your nose," "Scratch your head," and "Look behind you." They can also be used for OBE foreplay. Short, physical suggestions are much easier to transmit and have them receive than complex suggestions.

To Send a Telepathic Suggestion

1. Create the normal telepathic link as you did in "Making a Telepathic Connection".
2. Think of your suggestion and move that suggestion from your mind, through the white light and into their mind.
3. Make sure your suggestion is clear, concise, and simple. It helps if you send a picture, sound or idea with the suggestion, and not just the words.
4. Close the connection as you did in "Making a Telepathic Connection".

Allie's Example

To add to the previous telepathic connection example instead of just telling Will that I missed him, I would add in a suggestion of, "Visit me tonight." With that suggestion I would do my best to also send Will a picture of our favorite willow tree down by the river. This way he would know that when I want him to visit me tonight in our dreams, we would meet at our favorite willow tree.

Because he and I know each other so well we use shortcuts in our communications. If our connection was new, Will would have no idea what I meant by the willow tree by the river. I would have told him to meet me here, showed him the picture, and added in town names or landmarks so he could find the tree.

Yes, we would have met up in the dream world and not in the physical reality, but he would still need to find the tree in the dreamscape. Plus, being a guy, you know he wouldn't stop for directions. HA!

But Don't Take My Word For It

1. Do you have a partner? Set up a date and time for the two of you to connect. Keep the connection short and sweet. Note your impressions in a journal. Compare notes.

2. If you are single, connect to a person you do know: family member, best friend, current crush, or ex high school flame. Keep the connection short and sweet. It is easier to find out if you actually connected if you can pick up the phone and ask. Note your impressions in a journal.

3. Once you made a short connection with another person. Next try to send a telepathic suggestion. For example, for the other person to call, text, or send you an email.

Keep an open mind. Remember that nothing happens immediately. This takes practice.

Telepathic Foreplay

Like with the story of Lisa and Ben, have you ever had such an intense daydream that it caused you to become sexually aroused or to experience an orgasm? Experts say that the mind is the largest and most important erogenous zone on a human being. Since this is fact and not science fiction, it is conceivable that two people can connect via the energy body and minds to turn each other on to such a state that a physical orgasm is achievable from both partners.

Out of the three OBE sex methods - telepathic sex is the easiest to master.

Why? With telepathic sex, your conscious mind is actively engaged in the sexual event. Your brain waves connect with another's brain wave. In your mind's eye you can see, your temporal lobes enable you to hear, your taste buds come alive with taste, and your sensation of touch ignites with the feel of the sexual act, taking place.

It is easy to remember telepathic sex experiences, as your conscious mind is not separate for your physical body as it is in dream and astral sex. Instead, it still resides on the physical body with one's mental energy field making the sexual connection instead of the astral energy field. The person is awake, fully conscious with the sexual acts happening in real time. Telepathic sex can happen anytime, anywhere - on a plane, in the shower, in your bed, standing in line -- there are no limits to where it can take place! However, some people find it easier to achieve (at least at first) in a quiet environment.

Think of telepathic sex as real-time sex without the physical merging. With telepathic sex, the odds of having an orgasm are very high as none of your energy bodies (astral, mental, emotional - etc...) is separate from your physical body.

Can you tell if you make the connection with another person or if it is just a fantasy? Yes, you can. How? Just as you can tell with a telepathic communication - you have that zing of energy and a warm flow over your body when you have that telepathic connection. If this factor is missing in the telepathic sex, then you are simply having a fantasy and not the telepathic sex.

Just like with physical sex, there is foreplay in telepathic sex!

Telepathic Foreplay

Think of telepathic foreplay as a version of a telepathic suggestion. The connections are quick, to the point and always (obviously) involve some form of sexual foreplay.

The easiest and most effective foreplay methods include:

- Kissing the target person's neck
- Nibbling on or blowing into the target person's ears
- Giving the target person a quick flick of your tongue up the center of their back
- Playing with the target person's nipple – whether it's licking, sucking, nibbling or fondling
- A quick couple licks in the target person's groin
- Grabbing the target person's butt

How to Have Telepathic Foreplay

Remember, these acts are quick and to the point. You can do this while standing in line, puttering away at work or taking your shower!

- Close your eyes and telepathically connect to your sex partner. If you do not have anyone - imagine someone you know that you would like to have sex with.
- Once you have connected...hold it there for a minute.

- Pick a place on their body you would like to play with a bit. Pick one spot and one spot only.
- Once you pick the spot, imagine yourself dishing out the foreplay. Take in the sensation of their surprise and pleasure. Really feel what is going on with all of your senses. Do this for 30 seconds.
- Break the connection
- Repeat as needed throughout the day

For now, concentrate on one area of foreplay at a time. The more skilled you get in telepathic sex, the more foreplay you can add. When you do feel you are ready for more foreplay add something else to the mix, but again only stay on that area for 30 seconds. So if you are going to lick an ear – do it for 30 seconds and then move to the nipples – for 30 seconds for a grand total of 1 minute of foreplay.

More is not better here unless you know what you are doing. The last thing you want to do is turn off your target person to a sexual encounter with you.

The more time you can give the joy of telepathic foreplay, the more your target person will be aroused. This is a great way to get a partner revved up for an evening of physical sex, OBE sex or both!

But Don't Take My Word For It

1. Practice first with this telepathic exercise:

This works well if you already have a physical sex partner - it doesn't matter if they believe in OBE or telepathic sex - although it is helpful if they do.

A. Close your eyes and imagine your sex partner. If you do not have anyone - imagine someone you would like to have sex with that is within reason and accessible to talk to.

B. Once you have that person centered in your thoughts and you can really imagine them - how they talk, dress, look, smell, etc.....hold it there for a minute.

C. Make the telepathic connection.

D. Pick a place on their body you'd like to lick. Good spots are the center of the back, side on the neck, ear lobe. Try to keep the sexual places like nipples, clitoris, and penis for another time.

E. Once you pick the place, imagine yourself licking them there - repeatedly. Do this for 1 - 3 minutes.

F. Break the connection.

G. Note your impressions in a journal.

The next time you talk to them, find out in your own special way if it felt like something was licking their neck, ear, back and/or if they felt any sensations at all. If this was your sexual partner and you two agreed to do this, share experiences.

The goal of this exercise is to get you to telepathically connect - hold that connection - and perform a sexual act without it being overly sexual. The next time you try this - up the minutes and try a different part of their body (but keep it from being overly sexual).

2. Once you find success with the above exercise - try telepathic foreplay. Note your impressions in a journal.

Telepathic Sex

"Allie and Will"

It's early in the morning, earlier than I would ever want to be awake. But I'm working on my Atlantis book and the only time I can carve out to write is from 4:15 am to 6:30 am. Then it's taking care of the animals, a quick shower, and getting my son up for school.

Lately my showers had been anything but quick. Why? Will's energy kept showing up in them. When he's around, the last thing I want is quick.

This particular morning I knew Will arrived when I heard, "Good mornin' beautiful," spoken with a southern drawl that makes my heart race and my knees go weak. I was right in the middle of rinsing my hair. My breath caught in my throat when my nipples tingled from his touch. Not wanting this moment to end, I stayed under the shower, enjoying the nipple play.

I kept my eyes closed and enjoyed the sexual dance. I could feel his energy being pulled from me, as if there was something or someone demanding his attention. The tingling on my nipples lessened for several seconds and then with a resounding WOW - I could feel his kisses all over my body.

With each kiss a stronger zap of energy flowed through my body.

He pushed me against the wall, grabbed my legs and hoisted me up so that he could enter - thrusting deep and strong. The energy that surged through my body with each thrust was opening up all my chakras', primary and secondary, setting my body on "fire". Without touching myself at all, my orgasm swelled and released sending me into bliss. I felt a kiss on my cheek and he was gone.

Had this been physical reality, there is no way I the world he could have hoisted me up against the wall. I weigh more than he does. Not leaps and bounds more - but enough to make it difficult. With telepathic sex, Will and I are able to connect no matter where in the world either of us are physically located.

How to Have Telepathic Sex

As you can tell from the previous instructions on telepathic foreplay, telepathic sex is not hard to do. The hardest part is connecting and that is easier to do the more you practice at it.

Prearranged Partner Telepathic Sex

1. You and your partner set up a time and/or day you wish

to have telepathic sex. Discuss the setting - like your favorite place for sex - the beach, the shower, hot tub or in a four-poster bed or agree to surprise one another.

2. Decide on who will be the instigator - who will be the one to start the session.

3. Several minutes before the prearranged time, make sure that neither of you will have any disturbances. No phones, TV or email!

4. Quiet your mind. If you find that you are having distractions from the day, simply imagine a feather and sweep the thoughts out of your mind.

5. When you are ready to telepathically connect - imagine your partner in the predetermined location.

6. If you are the instigator, see your partner standing, back to you. Approach them and stop a few inches away. If you are not the instigator, then imagine yourself standing there - waiting.

7. You will know when the connection is a success if each of you will be able to feel the other person's presence and the energy involved. That is why it is important that one have their back to the other. When you sense that "feel" about the other person, you know that you have a solid connection. In addition, the individual indicators of light-headedness, vibrations in the sacral chakra, etc. Once the person standing senses the instigator behind them, he or she should turn around.

8. Imagine yourselves having sex with one another. Immerse yourself in the connection. Make sure you can absorb and FEEL the emotions/sensations associated with the energy union.

9. Allow yourselves to be in the moment. You will be able

to feel their lips on yours, hands all over each other's body, intercourse and more. It is sometimes tempting (at least at first) to cut off the connection during the sexual act because the sensations can be so real – and it freaks you out. Follow it through – you will thank yourself later!

10. After you have experienced an orgasm/ heightened sense of sexual arousal, close the connection.

If you and your partner were in the same building, it would be an excellent time to engage in physical sex. If separate, this was a great prelude to future physical sex.

Allie's Example

Will and I decided to meet up at 2:00 pm ET on Saturday. I would be the instigator and meet up in a Four Seasons hotel room. At 1:55 I got comfy and turned off any distracting items, such as phone and email. I quieted my mind by using a "floor broom" and sweeping away any lingering thoughts from the day.

When I felt ready, I closed my eyes and started the telepathic connection. I "saw" Will in the hotel room, his back to me. I stood there - silent - hoping he sensed I'm behind him. I could feel the sexual tension. Almost as if there was an invisible energy band binding us. My heart raced, I felt like I was on the verge of a panic attack. My heart chakra felt like we were going down the first hill of a very big roller coaster (think the stomach dropping effect but in the heart chakra). After what felt like an hour, but actually only a few seconds, he turned around.

He stood there, looked at me with that crooked smile on his face. He ENJOYED the sexual tension between us. Damn him. But since I was the instigator, I wasn't waiting around any longer.

I grabbed him and threw him back on the soft bed. Jumping on top of him, I crushed my lips to his. I could physically feel my nipples harden and increased wetness in my crotch. My heart rate increased; my breaths quickened. We wasted no time as hands roamed, nakedness occurred, and body parts merged and merged to an orgasmic conclusion!

When we broke the connection (the orgasm will do that), if I smoked I would have lit one up. Of course if he was physically here, I would have ran and torn his clothes off!

Spur Of the Moment Telepathic Sex

This one is always nice and erotic when you want to surprise your partner with telepathic sex. It is great foreplay for a later sex date.

1. Imagine the setting where you would like to have telepathic sex. See it with detail as you can.
2. Make sure that the distractions are off.
3. Center yourself – quiet your mind.
4. Imagine the target person – center them in your mind. See them – feel them emotionally – touch them.

5. Make the telepathic connection.
6. Bring the target person into the setting you had already imagined. You can do this by seeing the two of you only connected by the white light – and then slowly bring in the surrounding scene, almost as if you two were wheeled into the scenery.
7. Here you are the dominant one – you control the sexual experience.
8. Kiss, fondle, explore as you would in physical sex. Get into this experience – your energies have merged, ride the sexual wave of emotions. Feel their lips – smell their sexual excitement. They may not be physically in front of you – but they are in front of you energy wise.
9. Keep following the sexual wave to its peak.
10. When you have achieved your orgasm or have reached that point sexually where you wanted to be – you can close the connection.
11. It is always polite though to make sure your partner is satisfied before the connection is closed.

Allie's Example

The process would be the same for Will and I as it was in the previous example. The only differences here is that Will would be facing me when I arrived in the shared energy space and I "wheeled" us into a scene picked out by me.

Taking a paragraph from the above example and tweaking it a bit: *When I felt ready, I closed my eyes and started the telepathic connection. I "saw" Will standing in front of me. I could feel the sexual tension. Almost as if there was an invisible energy band binding us. My heart raced, I felt like I was on the verge of a panic attack. My heart chakra felt like we were going down the first hill of a very big roller coaster (think the stomach dropping effect but in the heart chakra). After what felt like an hour, but actually only a few seconds, I "wheeled" Will and me into a room at the Four Seasons.*

Everything before and after that paragraph in the previous example stayed the same.

Single Telepathic Sex

If you are currently single, this connection is for you.

1. Make sure that the distractions are off.
2. Center yourself – quiet your mind.
3. If you know the person, you want to connect to, imagine them. If you do not know whom you want to connect to, imagine the qualities you would like in a sex partner and/or future love interest.
4. Imagine the target person – center them in your mind. See them – feel them emotionally – touch them.
5. See the space around them, your ideal meeting place.

Try to bring it in as vivid as possible.

6. Make the telepathic connection.

7. Before you approach him or her, make sure he or she vibrates at the energy you want to be intimate with. Lower vibrations "feel" heavy. The higher the vibration, the lighter it "feels."

8. You are the dominant one – you control the sexual experience.

9. Introduce yourself to him/her.

10. Kiss, fondle, explore as you would in physical sex. Get into this experience – your energies have merged, ride the sexual wave of emotions. Feel their lips – smell their sexual excitement. They may not be physically in front of you – but they are in front of you energy wise.

11. As you engage in telepathic sex, allow the surrounding scene to unfold around you. Do not force a specific scene, let a scene organically unfold around the two of you.

12. Keep following the sexual wave to its peak.

13. When you have achieved your orgasm or have reached that point sexually where you wanted to be – you can close the connection.

14. Of course, it is always polite though to make sure your partner is satisfied before the connection is closed.

Allie's Example

I adore 6'4" broad-shouldered men with blue eyes and dark hair. Yummy! Plus, there is nothing sexier than a nice man who is kind and loves animals. So TV off, email and phone both off - check, check, and check!

I close my eyes and imagine a 6'4" blue-eyed hottie standing in front of me. His energy needs to be kind, caring, and love animals.

He's in a pair of white shorts, tan firm legs, and bare feet. Bare chested, sporting a Tom Selleck chest. His nose, cheekbones, and chin were rather fuzzy. I could not get them in focus. But at the end of the day it didn't really matter to me. I continued to push forward to make the telepathic connection.

I see him standing there. Well, not all of him, but enough to know that is whom I want to connect to. Before I approach, I double check his energy by being still and sensing to see if it is at the frequency I want. I know it's not a lower energy, because he doesn't "feel" heavy. He's light and has a faint sizzle telling me he vibrates at a higher frequency.

As I walk up to him, I see the scene build up around him. Nice white sand with blue-green water behind him. I slide my hands up his chest as I introduce myself. I like his lips. They taste salty. Kissing and fondling one another like high school kids, we slowly make our way to the water.

In the water we are as naked as can be. The water turns us both on something fierce. We enjoy each other's body/energy to a mutually satisfying end. I closed the connection.

If you are having problems connecting with someone pay attention to what you feel as the connection is trying to happen. Can you feel resistance? A tightness or even a "brick wall"? Maybe emptiness or nothing at all? This means that the person does not wish to connect to you. Respect their wishes and stop trying to connect.

But Don't Take My Word For It

1. Practice with the three telepathic sex methods. If applicable, share your experiences with your partner.

2. Note your experience in your journal.

CHAPTER FIVE:
Dream Sex

Has This Ever Happened To You?

"Hector and Lorraine"

Hector found himself in an unfamiliar multi-floor house. Everything around him was white; walls, furniture, floor, etc. With the area void of sound, Hector could hear his heart pounding so hard he thought it for sure was to jump from his chest. Hesitant, he investigated the first and second floors, finding no one. On the third floor he heard music. Slowly following the crisp sounds of a guitar, he turned the corner and found himself looking at his wife, Lorraine, taking a bath in a claw-foot tub.

"Join me," Lorraine asked.

The next thing Hector remembered he was naked in the tub with his wife. Kissing her all over while she methodically cleaned his penis with soap and water. The two moved in rhythm working their way to marital bliss when a beeping noise went off in the background. Hector knew it was the alarm clock, but if he could just stay in the dream just a few seconds longer…

No such luck. He woke up, turned off the alarm. When he wakes up, he usually has a hard-on. But this morning, his hard-on was accompanied by an intense sexual desire.

He looked over at his sleeping wife — the dream was so vivid. He could remember the feel of her skin, her touch, the temperature of the water, their intense lovemaking. He gently touched her face.

"We were having the most amazing bath," Lorraine purred.

Hector's mind raced. Did they have the same dream? How is that possible? He knew that if he said anything to his wife that the mood was shot as she'd want to talk about it. He did the only thing he could do at the moment; make love to his wife.

Hector and Lorraine compared dreams later that day. It was the same dream, but from two separate angles. Her dream started in the bathtub, he in the living room. After they found me and I taught them how to control their dreams, their sexy dreams happen often with their relationship reaping the benefits.

"Sarah"

Sarah found herself in the middle of the Italian Renaissance in the 15th century. She was helping a man put away paints. She was in an artist's studio and she assumed she was an assistant.

The next thing Sarah remembers was that she was rolling around naked on the floor with the artist, both of them rolling in paint and laughing their butts off. His hot kisses traveled from the tip of her nose, down her neck, teased her nipples, nipped at her stomach, and nestled in-between her legs. His tongue alternated between flicking her clit and probing her wetness. He was driving her crazy! All she wanted to do was scream in delight, but instead she woke up.

She couldn't believe she woke up. Looking at the clock it was only 2:21 am. Alone in bed, she knew she was too horny to fall back to sleep. After masturbating for a matter of minutes to achieve orgasm, she rolled over to think about that dream.

Who was he? Why could she still feel his kiss on her body? Remember the taste of his mouth? It seemed so real and vivid. She finally fell back to sleep about 3:30 am.

The dream bothered her for months. She told a few of her friends that it felt real and they thought she was nuts. That's when she found me. Upon reading the blog - she discovered that she wasn't the only one this has happened to. She was relieved that she wasn't crazy.

Dreamscape

Dreaming is a normal part of our sleeping life. Everyone dreams. Many people do not give a second thought to their dreams as they feel – after all – they are just dreams. Others do not give a hoot about dreams as they think that they do not dream – when it is actually that they do not remember dreaming.

In the vastness of our energetic connectedness, I wholeheartedly believe that our dreams are an inter-dimensional reality just like our waking reality. The difference being in our waking reality we have an automatic conscious control of our lives. In dreams, where control is possible, it is not an automatic conscious control.

Dreams are more important and more controllable than anyone thought possible 20, 10 even 5 years ago. With dreams, you can go anywhere, do anything, and be anyone.

It is all in how you perceive and control the Dreamscape.

What Is The Dreamscape?

An ever-changing collective dimension brought forth from the dreams, nightmares, and daydreams of all humans. The connectivity of the Dreamscape is to the past, present and future dimensions, astral layers, heaven, hell, the universe, and every dimension in between. When traveling the Dreamscape, the possibilities are endless.

There are a variety of steps to controlling the Dreamscape. You can still have dream sex without using all the steps. But using them gives you more control over what happens.

Dreamscape Steps:

1. Build dream portal and workstation.
2. Learn about dream recall.
3. Find your reality check.
4. Put it all together and lucid dream.

Dream Portal

What Is A Dream Portal?

As the oceans connect the continents, Dream Portals or doorways connect individual dreams together to form the Dreamscape. Whether we realize or not when we fall asleep and enter a dream, we enter that dream by going through a Dream Portal.

By recognizing the doorway and building our own Dream Portal, we are able to gain more control over our dreams right from the get go.

How to Build a Dream Portal

No two Dream Portals are the same. Each portal design is on an individual's likes, tastes, and overall general mood.

1. To construct your Dream Portal - sit and get comfortable.
2. Take out a journal or notebook and a pen.
3. Close your eyes and imagine yourself in a space where you feel comfortable and safe. It can be a place that is real or imagined, it does not matter as long as you feel comfortable being there.
4. Feel the emotions and feeling associated with this special place.

5. Once you have this place firmly embedded in your mind, open your eyes, and write about that place in as much detail as possible. This place is the *base* for your Dream Portal.
6. Now close your eyes once again and drift back to your base for the Dream Portal.
7. At the base, you will construct your portal. Make your unique portal from anything you can imagine: stone spirits, brick, glass, clouds, plants, trees, gold, precious stones, etc... Imagine the framework for your Dream Portal growing out of the ground and forming right before your eyes. The framework can be a circle, triangle, square, rectangle, etc…
8. Inside the framework, the doorway can have a door with a doorknob, energy, water, fire, etc… The doorway can be full of anything you can imagine water, stars, white noise, or be absent of everything.

You will travel through this Dream Portal as you drift off to sleep and enter the Dreamscape.

Allie's Example

I've gotten many requests on what my dream portal looks like. I'm a "Stargate" nerd. So yes, it looks like the Stargate SG1 portal, complete with "whoosh" sound and shimmery liquid-like surface when activated. But instead of it having symbols on it and made of some space metal (AKA Hollywood plastic), it is made from clear quartz crystal. It's quite cool looking if I do say so myself.

Dream Workstation

How to Build Your Dream Workspace

The Dream Workspace goes along side of the portal and helps you to achieve lucid dream status.

1. To construct your Dream Workspace - sit and get comfortable.
2. Take out the journal or notebook you used in to create your Dream Portal and a pen.
3. Close your eyes and imagine what your favorite workspace would look like. It could be a desk, alter, shelf, boulder, etc… anything that you would feel comfortable working with for lucid dreaming.
4. Once you have the image of your special workplace in your mind, write it in your journal in as much detail as possible.
5. Now close your eyes once again and drift back to your Dream Portal.
6. Just as your Dream Portal, your unique workplace can be made from anything you can imagine: stone spirits, brick, glass, clouds, plants, trees, gold, precious stones, etc... it can be made of the same material as your Dream Portal or not – it is completely up to you. Imagine the framework for your Dream Workspace growing out of the ground next to the Dream Portal (on either side) and forming right before your eyes.
7. If you wish, add accessories to the top of the Dream Workspace – your favorite crystals/stones, a picture, a map – whatever you feel is important to you. You can add or

subtract accessories to your Dream Workspace at any time.

8. This is the Dream Workspace where you will conduct any lucid dream work before you enter the Dreamscape.

Allie's Example

My workstation is an 1850's fireplace mantel made from quartz crystal instead of wood. If you ever watch any of my videos, the original fireplace is behind me in the frame.

Dream Recall

A key component of dreaming is the ability to recall your dreams. If you cannot recall your nighttime adventures – then there is no sense to travel the Dreamscape.

Dream Recall Tips

1. Before you go to bed, set up the intention of recalling your dreams.
2. Keep a dream journal/notebook and pen next to your head – or close to your head.
3. When you wake up, stay still.
4. Grab your journal and write down everything you can remember – no matter how small or insignificant the details might seem.
5. Write first. Speak to others, think about your day, pet the cat, or get up and go to the bathroom second.
6. As you go throughout your day, think back on your dreams and see if you can recall any more details. If you do- write them down.

Still having problems? Try this:

1. Set your alarm so that it will wake you up in the middle of a dream. Sure, it can be annoying at first – but most of the dreams that we remember take place right before we wake up. So if you wake yourself while you know you are dreaming (which usually is two hour before we are to wake up), you will be able to recall your dreams better.
2. You can set your alarm to go off 30 min before you are to wake up – and keep hitting the snooze button until you get

out of bed.

3. You can set your alarm to wake you a couple of hours after you go to sleep. After you write down your dream recall go to sleep.

Reality Check

When you lucid dream, you have to let yourself know that you are dreaming. How do you do this? By giving yourself realities check via a sign. This sign is something that you will train yourself to do in your dream so that you know you are dreaming.

Some examples of signs:

1. Looking at your right or left hand
2. Seeing a specific time on a clock i.e. 11:22
3. Hearing a bell
4. Smelling baking bread
5. A certain TV show or characters appear

When you see this sign – you ask yourself 'Am I dreaming" if you are dreaming – well obviously you will say yes. It helps if you practice this during the waking hours as well.

For instance if a certain time is your reality check, in your waking life when you see the clock display 11:22, you ask yourself "Am I dreaming?" This way you are forming the habit of asking, which will carry over to the dream world.

What do I use as my reality check? I look at my right hand.

Lucid Dreaming

What Is Lucid Dreaming?

Lucid dreaming is nothing more than being consciously aware that you are dreaming. To be involved in a lucid dream, you must realize while you are dreaming that you are doing just that – dreaming. When your awareness kicks in – the consciousness also does and therefore you are able to dictate the theme, direction, and tone of your dream.

Lucid dreaming is something that everyone can do. However, it takes patience and work to achieve lucid dreaming. In this world of "I want it now," many people give up after the first several attempts, as they are not getting instant gratification.

If you want something instant – text, send a tweet or hop on Facebook. If you want to explore endless possibilities – keep going!

Getting Started With Lucid Dreaming

1. Before you go to bed, make sure your dream journal and pen are within arm's reach.
2. Surround yourself with a bubble of white light for protection.
3. Lie still for a few minutes and formulate what you would like to see or do during your dreams. See this as vivid as you can.
4. Close your eyes. You are going to imagine yourself walking down a path towards your Dream Portal & Workspace. Construct this path from any material you want. The purpose of this path is to leave behind your waking life and to enter your dreaming life.
5. The length of the path depends on how your waking day went. If it was stressful, the path should be long (maybe taking 10 – 15 min to walk), if it was a mild day then make it a short path of maybe 5 min.
6. As you walk along, think about what you want to do in your dreams.
7. Do not be surprised if along the way you meet up with your guides and/or angels. They always like to be on the sidelines.
8. Go to your Dream Portal & Workspace.
9. On the workspace, mentally place any objects that deal

directly with the place or person you want to visit. If it is Paris, France, imagine yourself placing a small Eiffel Tower on the workspace. If it is a person, maybe place a picture of that person. When finished placing items on the workspace, the Dream Portal will activate.

10. Enter the Dream Portal and into the Dreamscape. By the time you step through the portal, you should be sound asleep.

11. When you are in the dream – give yourself the reality check. You can remind yourself to do this by placing it in the "what you want to do while dreaming" as you are walking down the path.

12. When you wake up, immediately write in your journal.

Lucid dreaming is not as difficult as people make it out to be. All it needs is practice and it will work. Everyone can do this – everyone.

Lucid dreaming will enable you to control the dream sex instead of it just happening to you.

But Don't Take My Word For It

1. Construct your Dream Portal & Workstation.
2. Decide on your reality check.
3. Buy a dream journal & pen. Put them both next to your bed. Use them!
4. Take a trip to the Dreamscape via a Lucid Dream.
5. Practice. Practice. Practice (seriously - practice).
6. Concentrate, recalling your dreams throughout the day. Write down any new information that arrives as you recall.

Dream Foreplay

Like Hector and Lorraine, or Sarah, do you remember a time or times in your life where you awoke from a vivid dream so sexually turned on that you had to find a release in order to fall back to sleep? Maybe you did not awake from a dream sexually turned on, but instead were already wet? Yes, I am talking about a wet dream. Guess what? You had dream sex and did not even know it!

Dream sex is the second easiest to master out of the three forms of OBE.

With dream sex, you are asleep with your astral energy body separating from your physical body and then off into the Dreamscape. Normally when you dream, your subconscious absorbs the adventures and keeps them stored in the fringe of your conscious memory, where they can filter in little by little into your consciousness. Everyone can learn how to Lucid Dream and engage in dream sex with the person or persons of choice. However, you do not have to know how to Lucid Dream in order to *engage* in dream sex! Only if you want to *control* the dream sex.

Dream sex is like astral sex, but you are asleep. With dream sex, the odds of having an orgasm are 50/50 as your astral energy body is separate from your physical body. However, the odds of you waking up sexually excited are very high. In fact, the odds of you not waking up needing a sexual release are very slim indeed. If you have a partner next to you in bed, he or she can benefit from your excessive sexual stimulation. If you are single, you can jump into solo exploration and have a very exhilarating release. Either way, you will have to find a way to have an orgasm if you expect to either fall back to sleep or get up and go about your day.

Dream Foreplay

Think of dream foreplay as a foreplay nap (only with a little more excitement). The connections are quick, to the point and always (obviously) involve some form of sexual foreplay.

The easiest and most effective foreplay methods are the same as telepathic foreplay:

1. Kissing the target person's neck
2. Nibbling on or blowing into the target person's ears
3. Giving the target person a quick flick of your tongue up the center of their back
4. Playing with the target person's nipple – whether

it's licking, sucking, nibbling or fondling

5. A quick couple of licks in the target person's groin

6. Grabbing the target person's butt

How to Have Dream Foreplay

Remember, these acts are quick and to the point. This is during naptime or maybe a quick nap before your actual bedtime. Dream foreplay should not last any longer than 20 minutes. This gives you time to fall asleep and to meet up with your sexual partner.

1. Set your alarm for 20 minutes. Can be shorter – but 20 minutes seems to do the job.

2. Envision where you want the dream foreplay to take place. Really imagine the surroundings, the sounds that are there and any smell that are present.

3. Place yourself in the white light bubble of protection.

4. Close your eyes and walk down your path to your Dream Portal/Workspace. As you walk the path, set the intent to do your reality check so that you can lucid dream. Mentally look over what foreplay you want to take place.

5. If you know the person, you are to meet up with, place a picture of them on the Dream Workspace. If you do not have a particular person - imagine

someone you would like to have sex with that is within reason (meaning leave celebrities alone). Place a list of their attributes (tall, dark hair, blue eyes, cute butt, etc.) on the workspace.

6. As you enter your Dream Portal mentally say their name.

7. Enjoy your foreplay. Remember – keep it simple, yet sensual and excitable – just like in the physical reality.

8. After you turn off your alarm, write down in your journal everything that you experienced.

For now concentrate on one area of foreplay at a time. The more skilled you get in dream sex, the more foreplay you can add. When you do feel you are ready for more foreplay add something else to the mix, but again only stay in the dream foreplay for 20 minutes tops.

But Don't Take My Word For It

Practice with dream foreplay more than once during the next seven days. If you find that you are having a difficult time remembering what happened, make sure you set your alarm. As soon as you awaken, pay attention to how you feel. Write in your journal what you remember.

Dream Sex

"Allie and Ted"

Ted arrived right at the start of my dreamtime and was following me from dream to dream until I would pay attention to him. When I woke up in between dreams, I could feel his energy essence still with me – I'd fall back to sleep and there he would be. I finally asked him "what" and he answered that he missed me.

With an arm swoop that would have made Rhett Butler proud, he planted a really soft, yet passionate kiss on me. In the next instant he must have changed the dream for we were in Dunshire Castle. Our home for so many years until that bitch burned it down with my son and I trapped inside. Ted and I were in our suite, on the big four-poster bed – which I realized was made of mahogany. His lovemaking style was very slow and deliberate. Different than times from the past several months when he seemed consumed with the final moments, instead of taking his own sweet time. His green eyes looked through me right into my soul, locking in and not wanting to let go. He smiled at me, cupped my face in his hands and entered me.

As soon as his penis entered, our energy shifted into a purplish/red glow, like a really cool sunset. With each thrust I could feel our energy expand and transform into a higher vibration. He whispered how much he loved me.

Imagine yourself on the highest roller coaster known to man, you're in the front seat, and you cannot see the bottom as you barrel down that first hill. That was how it felt when our energies merged. I awoke to still being incredibly turned on. Once that was taken care of, I remembered his touch, what it felt like to have him in me. I smiled and drifted back to sleep.

How to Have Dream Sex

As you can tell from the instructions on dream foreplay, dream sex is not hard to do. You just do in the Dreamscape what you would in reality. The nice thing with dream sex is that you can spice sex up a bit. Nothing is off limits if you both agree to it – or if you are single – the solo sky is the limit.

Basic Lucid Dream Sex

1. You and your partner set up a time to engage in dream sex. If single, skip this step.
2. Create the setting where you will meet. Make sure you get the details down – the easiest way to do that is to write it all in your dream journal.
3. If single, write in your journal the qualities you want

in your dream partner. If you know who the person is, write about him or her.

4. At the prearranged time (if with a partner), get comfortable and place the white light of protection bubble around you. If with a partner, he or she should do the same. Quiet your mind. If you find that you are having distractions from the day, simply imagine a feather and sweep the thoughts out of your mind.

5. Walk down your dream path towards your Dream Portal. Along the way, you might want to change into something sexy or simply strip off your clothes and be nude.

6. Think about what sexual acts you would like to do to your partner and to have done to you.

7. You may run into a spirit guide or two. They do not care that you are naked and thinking sexy thoughts. If you have any questions, ask them during this time.

8. When you reach the Dream Portal and Workspace – place on the workspace a picture of your partner (if you know what they look like) or a list of the qualities you are looking for in a partner.

9. Next to the picture, place items that would go along with the location i.e.: for the beach - a seashell, for the woods – a stick and/or pinecone, a swanky hotel – 800-thread count sheets, etc…

10. Once everything is on the workspace – the portal will activate and you can enter.

11. When you enter, use your reality check so that you are consciously aware that you are dreaming.

12. If your partner is not there upon entering the portal – call out to them, they will show up.

13. You and your partner will meet up and engage in the sexual experience.
14. You may want to set an alarm for an hour later so that you remember enough of your dream sex to write it down in your journal or notebook.
15. After you awaken and write in your journal, if your physical sexual partner is lying next to you - then you two can enjoy the physical fruits of your dream experience. If your partner is in another location, enjoy yourself as you remember the experience.

If you are trying to have dream sex with someone who is not your partner, but who you know, and you do not set this up ahead of time – you have to make sure to engage in the dream sex when you both are asleep. Sometimes this can get tricky if you are in different time zones. There is a way to connect with one asleep and one awake. However, it is outside the scope of these lessons.

Allie's Example

Ted - my devilishly handsome Brit is who I wanted spend some dreamtime sexing it up. Since he is in my soul group but not a person I can call up and say "Hey," there was no prearranged meet-up time. I took out my journal and wrote "Ted & Bathroom at Party," in the page's title space. I described the party and the lavish bathroom with a marble shower and a few shower heads. I put the journal aside and settled in.

My dream path always consists of a soft dirt path, void of stones. It twists and turns through a forest. I prefer to walk the path naked. The air feel great on my skin, the soil softly crunches beneath my bare feet. My mind is full of naughty thoughts about Ted!

On my way I am usually greeted by a few of my guides. Whoever is dominant in my energy at the time. As I strolled tonight, Joshua joined me. We chatted about a couple important topics until I came upon the opening of the path onto the beach.

Once on the beach, I moved to my dream portal and workstation. On the workstation I have pictures already of each of my guys from my soul group. So there isn't a need to put another picture of Ted there. But I did put a pair of wedding rings we wore in a past life. When the rings hit the workstation, the portal activated.

As I walked through, I fell asleep. Not sure how long after on the dreamscape that I looked at my reality check - my right hand - and answered that I was dreaming. I glanced around and did not see Ted. I called out to him.

The next thing I remember is being at a small party. He is sitting on a green couch that matches the color in his eyes. He has a beer in his hand. I'm holding a gin and tonic. I sit on the glass coffee table directly in front of him. I smile, thinking to myself, "How can I get him out of here?"

With that thought, he and I transferred to an outside picnic table, just he and I. In the background, I could hear the low murmur of the other guests. I got up from my side of the table and sat next to him. My thoughts turned to being alone and naked with Ted.

The next thing I remember is he and I are off in our meadow, naked, rolling around kissing one another. His hot breath on my left breast, his tongue teasing my nipple. My hands all over his body - sweat streaming down his chest.

He flipped me over on my stomach and entered from behind. Between his breath on my back and the strength that went into each thrust - the seemingly obvious conclusion was that we were headed for orgasmic climax. But then…

I woke up! Dang that alarm and my one hour experiment! After finishing off what the dream started, I wrote the details in my journal. The most vivid for me was the sweat on his chest and his breath on my back.

Simple Non-Lucid Dream Sex

If you wish to jump into dream sex without really being able to control the situation – your main objective is to meet up with the person and simply have sex. Try these easy steps.

1. Close your eyes and quiet your mind. If you find that you are having distractions from the day, simply imagine a feather or a floor broom and sweep the thoughts out of your mind.
2. Place the white light of protection around you.
3. Imagine your partner as vividly as possible. Your partner has to be forefront in your mind as you drift off to sleep. Keep repeating the details to yourself repeatedly as sleep overtakes you.
4. You and your partner will meet up and engage in the sexual experience.
5. You may want to set an alarm for 30 - 40 minutes so that you remember enough of your dream sex to write it down in your journal or notebook.
6. If your physical sexual partner is lying next to you - then you two can enjoy the physical fruits of your dream experience. If your partner is in another location, enjoy yourself as you remember the experience.

Allie's Experience

As I closed my eyes, I thought about an industrial sized floor broom going through my head and sweeping away all the crap of the day. With a new space void of outside events, I placed white light all around me, and my bed for good measure. With good energy dancing about, I brought **Vincent** into my imagination. I thought of his big ole teddy bear-ness, chocolate eyes, and fabulous smile.

I must have fell asleep, because the next thing I remember we are in a royal-looking bedroom suite. There is a four-poster bed with canopy. A plush red comforter adorned the bed. Looked to be crushed velvet; truly a bed for a royal couple.

We were on the bed. His lips teased mine. A small kiss, a nibble on my lips, then it would shift to a deeper kiss. Back again to teasing. The pattern continued for several minutes.

The scene changed to being on top of a windy mountain. The crunching beneath my naked backside turned out to be snow. But I wasn't cold. We were on our sides, he was behind, spooning me. His hands on my breasts teased my nipples with every thrust. I felt the sensations rising to an orgasmic conclusion. The point of orgasm, woke me up.

I didn't move thinking of what just happened. But my brain kicked in and said, "write it down or you'll forget." That's exactly what I did! The two items that stood out the most were the velvet comforter and the thrusting.

But Don't Take My Word For It

1. Engage in simple non-lucid dream sex at least once over the next week. Make sure you note your impression and write them in your journal.

2. Try basic lucid dream sex a couple of times over the next couple of weeks. If you have a problem remembering your dreams, go back over the dream recall and reality check sections. Make sure you note your impressions and write them in your journal.

CHAPTER SIX:
Astral Sex

Has This Ever Happened To You?

"Greg and Ellen"

Greg and Ellen meet often in the astral realms. They have been married for 5 years and love to add twists and turns to their relationship. It helps keep things hot and passionate.

When they met up at a posh house of prostitution in another dimension, Greg wanted to be a female and Ellen a male. Greg thought about growing breasts and a vagina. Once his thoughts centered on looking feminine, he looked the part. Ellen grew a penis.

In the midst of an astral orgy at the brothel, Ellen entered Greg from behind. Greg said he felt a surge of energy go up the middle of his body. It was like he plugged his vagina into an electrical outlet. Ellen felt an enormous boost of energy every time she thrust into Greg. Each time their energies merged, the energy in them and around them got stronger. Both commented that colors swirled all around them, like they were on an acid trip.

Greg spun around on Ellen's penis so that Greg now faced Ellen. The two merged and pulled apart in rhythm. The energy built with each moment that passed. The rest of the orgy members were nothing but a blur. Just when they thought they were going to reach orgasm, Greg disappeared. Ellen thought of her body and returned.

When she arrived, Greg was sitting up in bed. She asked what happened. He replied that he didn't know. With enough sexual energy to fuel a brothel, the two continued physically where they left off astrally. Except this time, they were both able to achieve an orgasmic conclusion.

"James"

James had been studying astral travel for about a year. He had many successful trips and just as many unsuccessful attempts. He found that if he awoke in the middle of the night, that this was when he was at optimal traveling energy. One night James woke up from his dream state. He looked at the clock, "3:35," it read. Half asleep, he thought back to the dream where he was with his deceased wife. He was getting tired of sharing his bed with his snoring dog. He hadn't tried to find someone when he took his astral trips. Maybe he should give it a try.

He decided he wanted someone laidback and passive like his deceased wife. She was a patient person who was open to life and all it had to offer. He had hoped he could find an astral lover with green eyes and brown hair, also like his deceased wife. He didn't want a clone, just someone close.

After astral separation, he thought of his wife. He couldn't help it. She had been on his mind. Next thing he knew he was underneath a waterfall. It reminded him of the waterfall from his honeymoon in Brazil. He looked around, enthralled with the beauty of it all. Off to his left his deceased wife glided in. He felt elated when he saw her. As he approached her, she shook her head no. She looked over to her left and faded away.

Heartbroken, he turned in the direction she looked. What he saw made his head spin. In front of him was a petite woman with green eyes and brown hair. Before his eyes she dissolved into a shimmering grayish-green energy mass. The green loved through the gray until they formed green eyes up to the top of what he supposed was the head.

She held out her "hand," which he hesitantly grabbed. As soon as they touched he thought for sure his hand, then his arm was on fire. He quickly took his hand back. She communicated with him telepathically not to be afraid. He thought he should "man up." So he did. He held out his hand. What happened next was a whirlwind of events.

The woman grabbed his hand and as soon as she touched him, they were away to a land with moving metal plates and silver goo running between the plates. The area was void of sound. Completely.

He went to open his mouth, and then realized he had no mouth. He was pure energy like his companion. She scooped some of the silver goo and motioned that she wanted to put it on him. He thought, "hell no." But he remembered that his wife brought him to her. He needed to trust.

He stepped towards her. In the blink of an eye she was in front of him; her energy inside his energy. The silver substance moved through his energy field that felt like Pop Rocks. With every micro-burst of energy he felt sexual excitement build. If he had a breath to catch, he wouldn't have been able to catch it. She pressed lips he couldn't see against his lips that he didn't know he had. The deeper the energy connection, the more his energy grew. The more his energy grew, the more intense the silvery goo's Pop Rocks feeling intensified.

She merged more of her energy. The energy was getting too great, too intense. Without thinking, he merged more of his energy with her. They were now halfway merged with one another. It took approximately 1/2 second before his energy body imploded, sending him slamming back into his physical body.

When his astral body merged with his physical body, he felt the bed groan under the weight. Opening his eyes, he had the mother of all erections. It took him only a few well-oiled strokes to orgasm. Exhausted, he fell right to sleep.

The next day he searched about astral sex and found - yep - yours truly. Once I explained to him what happened (it was his first astral sex experience) and how yes, it was his deceased wife…James has had endless fun and exploration (not to mention sex) in the astral realms.

Astral Travel

As humans, we have a countless desire for freedom. In the astral realms, it is all about freedom. You are able to travel anywhere, be anyone, and see anything at any time. The universe and its multidimensional existence is a non-stop sea of exploration. All you need to do to explore is learn how to astral travel.

What Is Astral Travel?

Astral projection occurs when your astral energy body separates, or projects, from your physical body. The astral projection turns into astral travel as the astral body travels the astral layers. The astral body does not have limits like the physical body. When the astral body gets to roam, it can roam anywhere it deems necessary: to the moon, another solar system, the past, a visit to the present realty, a future glimpse, the layers of the heavens or the layers of hell.

While the astral body is traveling, it can assume any shape, size, race, or gender it chooses. It can look like the physical body, ET, or Morris the cat. Communications are simplified and carried out telepathically. The art of travel is just as simple – think of where you want to go and you are there in an instant.

What Happens During An Astral Projection?

During an astral projection, the astral body separates from the physical body while consciousness shifts from your physical body into your astral body. The shift of consciousness happens so that you are able to remember your experiences. Without that shift in consciousness, your experiences would be lost to your conscious mind and could only be retrievable with deep meditation or hypnosis.

When astral projection occurs, a silver cord anchors your astral body to your physical body. So no matter where you travel or who you see, there is no danger of being separated from your physical body and never being able to return.

To end the astral projection and travel, all one has to do is think about the physical body and you immediately return.

Stages of an Astral Projection

1. **Vibrational Stage** – In this first stage, energy vibrations flood the body. Many people hear buzzing, humming, and sometimes even a roaring sound in their ears. Occasionally, a person will lose the ability to move or the body feels numb. The intensity of the vibrations and sounds can be all over the map – from low and calm to intense and frightening. It is during this vibrational stage that the consciousness shifts from the physical body to the astral body. The vibration and sounds are our conscious recognition of the high

frequency astral energy body as it separates from the lower frequency of the physical body.

2. **Separation Stage** – When the astral energy body separates, there is usually a general feeling of lifting, floating, or rolling out of the physical body. After the separation is complete, the vibrations and sounds cease.

3. **Exploration Stage** – Now that the astral body is a separate, yet connected entity it is time to explore the environment. The astral energy body is a high-frequency version of the physical body. It does not have to look like the physical body, but most people prefer to keep it that way. Because of the high-frequency construction, the astral body is thought response. The astral body can "think" its way to run, walk, float, or fly anywhere in the universe. To allow time for exploration, focus needs to be kept within the astral body and the current environment. It is good to note that when the astral body separates – the current astral layer world will be an exact replica of the physical world. Therefore, if it is raining out – it is raining in the astral world. Daylight and sunny in the physical world translates to the same sunlight in the astral world.

4. **Reentry Stage** – The rejoining of the astral body with the physical body happens automatically by simply thinking of the physical body. Sometimes during reentry, a person will experience temporary vibrations, numbness, and the inability to move. The sensations fade quickly as the bodies reunite.

Basic Astral Separation Methods

To separate using any of these methods, you will have to imagine that an exact double of you (right down to your underwear if you have any on) separates from your body. There will be an energy you that is the exact double of the physical you.

You will probably have to experiment to discover which method works best. All the methods take place after you recognize that the vibrational state (as discussed in the last part) is in full swing.

1. **Floating Out**: Focus in on the sensation of floating and allow your astral body to drift up and away from your physical body.

2. **Sit Up**: Focus in on your astral body sitting up and moving out of your physical body.

3. **Rolling Out**: Out of all the separation methods, this one is the most successfully used. Simply have your astral body do a sideways roll out of your physical body.

4. **Pull Yourself Out**: Focus on your astral energy body's arm extending out and your astral hand grabbing onto some sort of a large object – keeping in mind that the astral body is not limited by distance. Your astral arm could very easily reach across the room to your dresser. Once your astral arm/hand makes contact with the object, pull your astral body from your physical body.

5. **Climbing Out**: Imagine that there is a large and heavy rope (the kind you would have climbed in gym class) hanging down from the ceiling. With your astral energy hands, grab onto that rope and climb upwards – this pulls your astral body from your physical body.

6. **Top of The Head**: Focus in on your astral body separating from your physical body via the top of your head. Remember "I Dream of Jeanie" and the way the steam would come out of the bottle before Jeanie did? That is how your astral energy body will look like as it is coming out of your physical body from the top of your head.

7. **Divine Aid**: Reach out your astral hand and request aid from a guide, angel, or a deceased loved one. They will respond by grabbing your astral hand and pulling your astral body from your physical body.

Travel Techniques for Astral Projection

Use the techniques described in the previous lesson to get you to this point.

1. Separate your astral energy body from your physical body by using one of the Separation Methods above.

2. As soon as your astral body is out – things will look fuzzy, out of focus. To clear this up, command in a firm tone: "Clarity Now!" Things will clear up around you immediately.

3. Do not look back at your physical body – if you do, you will pop right back in it.

4. Think about where you want to go and/or whom you want to see. Your thoughts will take you immediately where you want to be.

5. When you are done with your travels – simply think about your physical body and you will return to it promptly.

6. Write down your experiences immediately in your journal/notebook.

When you astral travel you will encounter energy from all forms of life. Some will be human, some animals, while others have no shape at all or appear to look alien in appearance. There are also varieties of forms of energy. You will encounter positive and negative vibrations. If something does not feel right, then think of another place to go or your physical body.

Astral Travel/Projection Resources

There is so much more to learn about astral travel/projection than I can put in this book. I highly suggest you check out the resources below.

Robert Bruce: http://www.AstralDynamics.com

William Buhlman: http://www.out-of-body.com/

But Don't Take My Word for It

1. Do the energy exercises from the section on increasing your energy fields, before you try to astral travel. The exercises will raise your vibrations making it easier to take off and land.

2. Practice several, if not all, of the separation techniques to see which one works best for you.

3. Try to astral travel from astral projection to reentry. Remember that once you separate, yell "Clarity Now." Next, think of a place you would like to visit. It can be Aunt Sue's house, when Lincoln was assassinated, or to visit a deceased friend or relative. When you are done, do what Dorothy did in the "Wizard of Oz" – 'There is no place like home.' Instead of clicking your heels together, think of your body.

4. Make note of your impressions in your journal.

This takes time to master. Do not give up after the first few attempts. It is well worth it to push forward.

Astral Foreplay

Are you ready to learn how to experience the volcanic eruption of an energetic orgasm?

Astral sex is the hardest to master out of the three forms of OBE. The reasons for this are obvious if you tried your hand at the previous course: separating & remembering. Once you master those two things, astral sex is a piece of cake.

Astral sex is like dream sex, but you are awake. Like with dream sex, the odds of having an orgasm are 50/50 as your astral energy body is separate from your physical body. However, after you return the odds of you being sexually excited is very high. In fact, the odds of you not coming back and needing a sexual release are very slim indeed. If you have a partner they can benefit from your excessive sexual stimulation. On the other hand, if you are single, you can jump into solo exploration and have a very exhilarating release.

With astral sex, you are to become sexually aroused and engage in energetic sex with another energy. This energy can be a human or an energy from a faraway world. In the astral state, energy manipulates to a point where it feels and looks like physical body parts are merging -- but they are only energy and not actual physical parts.

However, humans are used to seeing a penis and vagina. Since the astral body reacts with thought, if you think you have a vagina or penis, you will display one.

What is actually happening is the throat chakra's are opening, expanding – which causes the other chakra's to open and enlarge one by one to engulf you both into one energized bubble.

Astral Foreplay

Sometimes when people see a ghost, what they are actually seeing is the astral body of a live person who is on the present (some call it reality) plane. This is where astral foreplay takes place – on the present/reality plane with the projector (you) on the plane and the foreplay target in the physical.

The easiest and most effective foreplay methods are almost the same as telepathic & dream foreplay:

1. Kissing the target person's neck.
2. Nibbling on or blowing into the target person's ears.
3. Caressing their face.
4. Giving the target person a quick flick of your tongue up the center of their back.
5. Running your hands up their chest.

6. Playing with the target person's nipple – whether it's licking, sucking, nibbling or fondling.
7. A quick couple of licks in the target person's groin.
8. Grabbing the target person's butt.
9. Walking right through the target person. This will "zap" them with energy as it will you.

How to Have Astral Foreplay

Foreplay is quick and to the point. Astral foreplay should last no longer than 5 - 10 minutes - total. However, the number of times you engage in astral foreplay within a 24-hour period is the projector's choice.

Rules apply when it comes to personal space – if you do not know a person or if this person does not want to have anything to do with you, then invading their space is taboo. What you do in the astral world has karma attached to it as it does in the physical world. Celebrities and high profile people are off limits. You can never say that I did not try to warn you.

1. Set your alarm for 5 or 10 minutes.
2. Place a white light protection bubble around you.
3. Envision the target person – imagine everything about them; how the look, smell, act and even taste.
4. Relax and enter into an astral projection.

5. Remember to say, "Clarity Now!"

6. Think of the target person – you will go immediately to them.

7. Engage in foreplay as if you were standing there in physical form. The target person may be able to get a glimpse of your astral body – but more times than not they will just be able to feel someone. Remember – keep it simple, yet sensual and excitable –just like in the physical reality.

8. When your alarm goes off – you will go directly back to your physical body. Write in your journal everything that you experienced.

For now, concentrate on one area of foreplay at a time. The more skilled you get in astral sex, the more foreplay you can add. When you do feel you are ready for more foreplay add something else to the mix, but again only stay in the astral foreplay for 5 - 10 minutes at a time.

But Don't Take My Word for It

1. Once you have mastered astral travel, give astral foreplay a try. Remember it is short, quick, and uncomplicated.

2. Provided you have a willing partner or you know someone who would not freak out if he or she thought a spirit was making moves on them – try astral foreplay with you in the astral levels and he or she still physically planted.

Astral Sex

"Allie and Bill"

My astral body split from my physical body. With one quick thought of Bill - I was transported directly to him on the real plane. He was sitting in a chair in a hotel room, lost in thought as he looked out the window. He sensed I was there - closed his eyes and there was his astral body before me.

Our energies merged into one and I could "hear" him tell me to hold on. In an instant we were inside of a very large crystal temple. This temple's energy field seemed to flux with our energy. I knew he had brought me home, to Atlantis. It seemed like we floated over to a clear pool of water. The crystal temple pulsated with our energy.

Off to the left I could sense other energy bodies watching us - to the right the same. This observation didn't both either one of us. Our energy merged with the water in the pool. From my energy field came a very strong red energy that stretched to Bill and encased him. From Bill emitted a violet or deep purple energy that went in my crown chakra, went straight down through my energy field - back over to the bottom of Bill's energy, up through the crown and over to me again so that it was a constant loop of energy.

The only way I can put this is that it felt alive - we felt alive - connected in every sense of the word. In the astral plane you can be a ball of energy or you can morph into a physical - looking body. What was really odd is that our heads and upper bodies morphed into our naked physical selves, but the bottom halves stayed as energy.

Bill grabbed the back of my head with his hands and brought his lips to touch mine. I can still feel the warmth of his tongue. As our tongues danced as one, his left hand lowered to play with my already erect nipple. As pleasure coursed through us, I could hear him ask if I was ready -- and I assured him that I was. Our lower energy halves merged into one. It was such a jolt of combined energy that we both had a hard time holding on to one another to keep the connection. Within milliseconds we were both having an energetic orgasmic climax. As we orgasm over and over again - I could tell that the energy of the crystal temple was so high that it was brighter than any star seen by the naked eye.

Then I felt like I was falling, felt the bed give way as if I've fallen from the sky -- and I opened my eyes.

My physical body was soaked in every way possible. There was no need to finish anything off as it was finished not only astrally, but physically as well.

I washed up, went to bed and almost immediately to sleep where I stayed asleep for over 8 hours. I woke up feeling very refreshed.

How to Have Astral Sex

As you can tell from the directions on astral foreplay – the hardest part of astral sex is the separating and then the remembering. With astral sex, you can be either gender. Therefore, if you are female in the physical plane, you can be a male in the astral plane – and vice versa.

Astral sex takes place on the astral plane. Be respectful. If someone does not want to engage in sex with you, go somewhere else.

Astral Sex Methods

Single Sex with an Astral Lover/Kindred Spirit

Before you travel, have in mind the attributes of your astral lover (eye color, height, personality, etc…)

1. Place the while light protection bubble around you.

2. Relax and separate your astral energy body from your physical body.

3. As soon as you arrive on the astral plane, say "Clarity Now!"

4. Send out thoughts of the attributes of your kindred sexual spirit.

5. Once your astral lover arrives – do not immediately jump into astral sex. Tune into his or her energy and make sure it is energy you want to be intimate with. Low energy gives off muted, heavy vibrations. Higher energy gives off light, but strong vibrations. If it is an energy you want continue to the next step. If not, think of your physical body and go back.

6. Embrace one another; get comfortable being in each other's energy.

7. While in the embrace, if you want to move to a specific location, think of it now and you'll both go there.

8. **When you are ready to engage in astral sex, face one another. Line up your ever-expanding throat chakras. One by one, concentrate on your chakras opening up – starting from the root chakra (at the base of your spine) all the way up to your crown.

9. Slowly, move towards one another until your energy bodies are touching. You should see a swirl of light around you, as if you are in a white tornado. This white light emits from a higher-level chakra to engulf the two of you and make you one.

10. Enjoy the explosive experiences – taking note of the colors around you as well as the amount of energy that moves through your energy body.

11. The energy can be soothing or it can be highly intense.

12. One of two things will happen here – either your physical body is going to react immediately to your astral experience or you or your astral sex partner will enjoy the energy and say good-bye. If you do not go back immediately to your body – think of your physical body and you will return.

13. Write down your experiences immediately in your journal/notebook.

14. If you find that, you are still sexually turned on – snuggle up to your physical partner or have fun in solo exploration.

15. If you find that you enjoyed this experience with that particular astral sex partner, the next time you want to engage in sex with them, think about their energy the next time you astral travel. This is why it is nice to get to know something about them so that it is easier to find them again if you want to.

Single Sex with a Specific Astral Lover

Your specific astral lover can be a person that you are already in a relationship with or not.

1. Place the while light protection bubble around you.

2. Relax and separate your astral energy body from your physical body.

3. As soon as you arrive on the astral plane, say "Clarity Now!"

4. Send out a thought about your specific person.

5. You will either immediately travel to them or they will travel to you.

6. If this is your first time meeting up with this specific person, embrace one another; get comfortable being in each other's energy.

7. **When you are ready to engage in astral sex, face one another. Line up your ever-expanding throat chakras. One by one, concentrate on your chakra's opening up – starting from the root chakra (at the base of your spine) all the way up to your crown.

8. Slowly, move towards one another until your energy bodies are touching. You should see a swirl of light around you, as if you are in a white tornado. This white light emits from a higher-level chakra to engulf the two of you and make you one.

9. Enjoy the explosive experiences – taking note of the colors around you as well as the amount of energy that moves through your energy body.

10. The energy can be soothing or it can be highly intense.

11. One of two things will happen here – either your physical body is going to react immediately to your astral experience or you or your astral sex partner will enjoy the energy and say good-bye. If you do not go back immediately to your body – think of your physical body and you will return.

12. Write down your experiences immediately in your journal/notebook.
13. If you find that you are still sexually turned on – snuggle up to your physical partner or have fun in solo exploration.

You can engage in astral sex the way you would with physical sex with the kissing, fondling, hugging, cuddling, and penetration. The chakras will open up one by one automatically as you engage in astral sex. But one way or another, the energy bodies will become one – and that is when the fireworks go off

Allie's Example

Getting ready to astral travel, I placed the white light of protection around me. I relaxed and after a few minutes heard a buzzing in my ears with my stomach doing flip flops. I knew this was the point of separation. Using the rolling out method, my astral body separated from my physical body.

When I separated my body, I yelled, “Clarity now!” Around me it was very bright - almost as if I had a spotlight shining right in my eyes and I couldn't see. Part of it made sense as it was the middle of the afternoon. But the sun was behind the place my energy separated. Still, I did not let curiosity get the better of me. I knew better than to turn around and look at my physical body, so I thought about Bill -- and there he was.

He held out his hand and I took it. We immediately went to the moon. I found this to be very odd since I couldn’t remember going to the moon before. So here we were, two energy masses floating on the moon. Bill's right hand turned into what I would describe as a clit licking sex toy. But instead of placing it where one would think to - on the clit, he slid it inside my energy body. It was such an odd, yet exciting feeling. It felt like someone stroked my energy body from the inside out. It was highly erotic and tantalizing. I felt myself getting lighter. I thought that I couldn't take it anymore. That's all I had to do was think about it, that the excitement was getting to me. Bill took the cue.

He positioned his energy so that his chakra’s lined up with my chakras. One by one our chakra’s expanded until we were in an energy vortex, swirling with white energy. Our energy peaked.

Immediately, it felt like I was going down the largest roller coaster in the world, in the front seat with no seat belt on and at the same time someone shoving a coffee IV into my arm. It was almost too much.

Right when it felt like I was bursting free with an astral orgasm - I shot back to my body. I found myself not quite finished. I knew there was no way I could go through the rest of my day like this. Thankfully, I had a previous job as a sex toy tester. Gave me various options to choose from!

Note: Had I not a specific person in mind, like Bill, in step 4 I would have thought of a blue-eyed male, sensual and artistic, who helped everyone he met.

Relationship/Partner Astral Sex

You can have partner astral sex either before or after engaging in physical sex with that partner. The easiest time for anyone to have an astral projection is immediately following an orgasm.

Before A Physical Orgasm

1. You and your physical partner set up a time to astral travel. If you want to go to a location on the astral plane that is special to the two of you – remember to arrange it before your projection.
2. Set your alarm for 10 to 20 min. The more you do

this, the longer you can stay in the astral realm.

3. Naked, lie next to one another in bed or on the floor.

4. Place the white light of protection around the two of you.

5. Relax and separate your astral energy bodies from your physical bodies. It is nice if the projection is simultaneously – but it is not necessary.

6. As soon as you arrive on the astral plane, say "Clarity Now!"

7. Once you are both on the astral plane, hold hands and go to the predetermined special place. If no place was prearranged – one of you decides the location – but make sure you are holding hands so that you travel together.

8. Explore one another. Use your imagination. Merge your hands with one another. Touch and notice how your energy races. Engage in astral foreplay. Be creative.

9. If the alarm hasn't gone off yet, slowly, move towards one another until your energy bodies are touching. You should see a swirl of light around you, as if you are in a white tornado. This white light emits from a higher chakra to engulf the two of you and make you one.

10. Enjoy the explosive experiences – taking note of the colors around you as well as the amount of energy that moves through your energy body. The energy can be soothing or intense. But since you two have a history together, there is added energy involved thereby probably making this an intense

encounter.

11. If the two of you wanted the type of astral sex that makes your toes curl, walk into one another and be one instead of becoming one. There is a difference. If you are one by occupying the same space with combined energy – the result is explosive enough to send you straight back to your physical bodies.

12. Once either the alarm goes off or astral orgasms send you back to your physical bodies, take advantage of your heightened energy for hot, erotic physical sex.

13. When you emerge from your orgasmic coma, write down your experiences/impressions in your journal.

Allie's Example

Owen and I decided to have astral sex at 8 pm that night. We wanted to go to a futuristic hotel with floating, round, rooms.

At 7:57, we set the alarm for 20 min and put our naked bodied on the bed. We put the white light of protection around us. Upon the separation of our astral bodies from our physical bodies, we both said "Clarity now!" We held hands and went off to the futuristic hotel.

We explored one another. Touching with a finger on a shoulder, then moving a hand inside of the energy to tease and excite. We took turns with one another - teasing, driving each other crazy.

We moved to one another so that our energies barely merged with one another. As the white light swirled around us, our energy levels soared. It felt like we were in an energetic cloud. But the emery wasn't soft like a cloud, it was spicy and "on." I had a feeling that the alarm was about to go off; so, I walked into his energy so that we merged into one. That explosive merging felt as if a volcano erupted from within. It sent us right back to our bodies.

We landed back in our physical bodies, took a few moments to let it sink it. The sexual sensations were still there. Owen rolled onto me and our sexual exploits continued.

After A Physical Orgasm

This needs to take place with both of your physical bodies in the same room having sex with one another.

1. Delay climax for as long as possible. Only allow the release when you can no longer hold it back.
2. Immediately following the orgasm (with practice – during the orgasm), separate your astral body from your physical body.

3. As soon as both of your astral bodies are out – step or roll into one another – and hold on. Explosive orgasmic fireworks will ensue!

Allie's Example

Continuing on from the previous example, Owen and I are engaged in steamy, physical sex. With each thrust we are reaching closer and closer to orgasm. We both tried to keep our mind off of the pure pleasure we felt.

We hit a point where we couldn't take it any longer. I hit orgasm and then he did. As we were going through the rise and fall of the orgasmic energy, we separated our astral body from our physical body.

As soon as the separation occurred, we merged our astral bodies into one. Our astral orgasms extended our physical orgasms. It was one hell of a ride!

But Don't Take My Word for It

1. Once you feel comfortable with astral foreplay, try astral sex. Each person has a slightly different perspective on the experience. Why? Because the astral body is thought oriented. Our thoughts are shaped by our life experiences, personality, and perspective. If you and your partner have different experiences during the same session, that is normal. If you have a partner, discuss the astral experience. If you met up with an astral lover, just enjoy the ride.

2. Note your impressions in your journal.

CHAPTER SEVEN:
OBE Sex Protection

OBE Protection Methods

Mediums have the problem of once the spirit world realizes that he or she can communicate with them, word spreads like wildfire. It also happens when you engage in OBE sex. Once you have some experience with energy sex, your energy body expands and strengthens. That strength causes your inner light to grow. Energy attracts energy. Word will get out that you can engage in energy sex and energy bodies will line up to have a chance with you.

Unknown energy bothering you is not the norm. But it does happen. That is why I decided to add this section to the course. You have only been engaging in OBE sex for eight weeks now and should not yet be on the OBE radar. I considered putting this in with each section just in case you encountered any trouble early on. However, I felt that it was information overload. The white light protection I suggested for you to do should have been plenty.

Introduction

As you are using OBE and telepathically connecting, exploring the Dreamscape and traveling the astral layers, you will from time to time, come across unwanted energies. The energies could be trying to invade your personal space and grab some telepathic sex, invade your dreams and try to seduce you into dream sex or try to move inside your energy bubble in the astral layers for explosive sex.

The same rules apply during OBE experiences as they do in the physical reality. But just as there are people on the physical plane who do not know how to take "No" for an answer – there are those in OBE world with that same problem.

So when NO will not work alone – try some of these protective measure to shield your space from other souls.

Telepathic Protection

You'll know when you need this – a person keeps entering your mind who do you do want there. You'll know they are there by your constant thoughts of them. If it is sex that they want, you'll be able to feel them on your body and your body will respond. Usually if it is someone you do not know or want – the body responds with an allover "icky" feeling. Plus thoughts of kissing or have sexual relationship with this person will pop into your head and you know darn well that those thoughts were not put there by you.

All humans are born with a natural protective force field around them. But sometimes you need some extra help.

Telepathic protection methods:

1. **Simple**: Tell the energy "No" in a stern and commanding voice. This is always your first line of protection/defense.
2. **Basic Wall**: Tell the energy "No" in a stern and commanding voice while simultaneously imagining a steel circular wall clamping down around you. It helps if you can imagine hearing the "clink or clank" of the steel wall moving into place.
3. **Intermediate Wall**: Imagine either a wall of fire or of nails (with the sharp end pointing out) around you as protection. If they do not move away – imagine either the fire chasing them or the nails flying out in all direction to puncture them.

4. **Advanced Wall**: The more you practice telepathic sex, the more you will put out an unseen vibe that you enjoy telepathic sex. This attracts a lot of low life energy to you – since you are not a telepathic lady/lord of the evening, you'll need a reinforced wall that is there 24/7.

   You can transform this wall to let certain energies/people in, while keeping the rest out:

   A. Imagine a wall growing up out of the ground, surrounding you, and climbing until it reaches over your head and locks together. So that you are in encased in an upside down energy test tube (for lack of a better way to describe it). This wall can be out of any material you like - a good material is a nice thick ice wall so that light can still shine through.

   B. Now in this wall you can cut doors for as many people that you would like to let through to contact you.

   C. Over each door, put something that is characteristic to each energy that is allowed to come to you. Could be a name, a job, physical characteristic, their voice, etc... When you are imagining whatever characteristic it is over each door, really imagine that soul's energy and allow the emotions that this particular energy brings you to permeate your body. Once those intense feelings are gone - you know that the doorway is programmed for that energy only to pass through.

   D. If someone falls out of favor with you - then you can imagine yourself tearing out there door. Or if someone else comes along later- you can add their door.

5. **The Hail Mary Wall**: This wall is used when nothing else will work:

   A. Imagine a wall growing up out of the ground – a few

feet from you - surrounding you, and climbing until it reaches over your head and locks together. Make this wall out of metal spears or nails with the pointy ends facing outward.

B. Between you and that wall, place a moat. Yes, a moat that would have surrounded a castle in the dark ages.

C. Imagine a wall growing up out of the ground, surrounding you, and climbing until it reaches over your head and locks together. So that you are in encased in an upside down energy test tube (for lack of a better way to describe it). This wall can be out of any material you like - a good material is a nice thick ice wall so that light can still shine through.

D. Over each door, put something that is characteristic to each energy that is allowed to come to you. Could be a name, a job, physical characteristic, their voice, etc... When you are imagining whatever characteristic it is over each door, really imagine that soul's energy and allow the emotions that this particular energy brings you to permeate your body. Once those intense feelings are gone - you know that the doorway is programmed for that energy only to pass through.

E. If someone falls out of favor with you - then you can imagine yourself tearing out there door. Or if someone else comes along later- you can add their door.

Now with the above **Hail Mary Wall** – if you want even more protection, you can add a group of KNIGHTS in between Steps B & C. With all of the above methods, you do not have to be thinking about it all the time. When you want the protection reinforced, recreate the boundaries.

Dream and Astral Protection

Since when we dream, we astral project – the projection methods for dream protection and astral protection are the same.

1. **Simple**: Tell the energy "No" in a stern and commanding voice. This is always your first line of protection/defense.

2. **Passive Environmental**: Placing objects in your physical environment help to keep unwanted energies at bay:
   A) *A small indoor fountain* – this can be placed by your front door or by the door to your OBE room/bedroom (where you dream and/or astral project).

   B) *A ring of salt*: place salt around your bed, or where you OBE project from before your projection/dream. You can also place salt around your home (inside or out) either directly on the floor, or in sachets. Replace once a week if needed.

   C) *Holy water*: this can be obtained from churches. Sprinkle some on your body before you dream or astral project.

   D) *Bowls of water*: Fill non-metal bowls with clean (preferably spring water) water and place one bowl at the foot of your bed and one at the head (for dreams) or place on in front and behind you or your OBE furniture before you astral project.

   E) *Garlic*: peel and slice a few cloves of garlic

into thin slices. Spread the garlic over several small plates. Place the plates at the head & foot of your bed, night stand and/or underneath the bed (for dreaming) and around your OBE furniture before you astral project.

3. **Aggressive In-World**: Use these methods if someone shows up and will not leave you alone during a dream or astral travel:

   A) *Protective Ball*: Imagine an energy field of white light surrounding you so that you are in a protective ball. No harm can come to you from inside here.

   B) *Protective Armor*: Imagine yourself protected by a glowing white light suit of armor, complete with a shield. This is an impenetrable force.

   C) *Sword Protection*: Imagine wielding a powerful lightning bolt or white light sword. Create the sword out of something that you will not have to put a lot of thought into. For example if you were a *Lord of the Rings* fan – you could imagine a sword. If you were an avid cook – it could be a pan/pot of light or a writer – a mighty pen of light.

   D) *Explosive Protection*: Imagine that you have a grenade in your hand. When you throw it, the area will burst into a brilliant white light removing any unwanted energy from your path.

You can combine the protection methods to find out which suits you the best. Whatever you do, it has to be something that does not require a lot of thought if you are already dreaming or astral traveling.

CHAPTER EIGHT:

OBE Sex Grids

Grids for Better OBE Sex

Sometimes it is nice to have a little boost of energy when engaging in OBE or OBE sex. It helps to make the connection stronger, the dream deeper, and the travel easier. All of the below grids I have used personally! Use them - trial and error. If it's too strong, remove stones. Too weak, add stones. Everyone's energy is different and therefore, everyone will react different to the grid's energy.

Most of the grids are designed to be placed under your bed. If you're like me and have cats, place the grid inside of a box with a lid. This way the fur babies will not play soccer with your stones.

OBE Sex Grid with Rubies

Supplies:

3 Terminated Quartz Crystals (Q)

3 Rubies (can be rough) (R)

3 Carnelian (C)

Working from the outside in Quartz 1st, then Ruby, finally Carnelian), with the terminations pointed towards you:

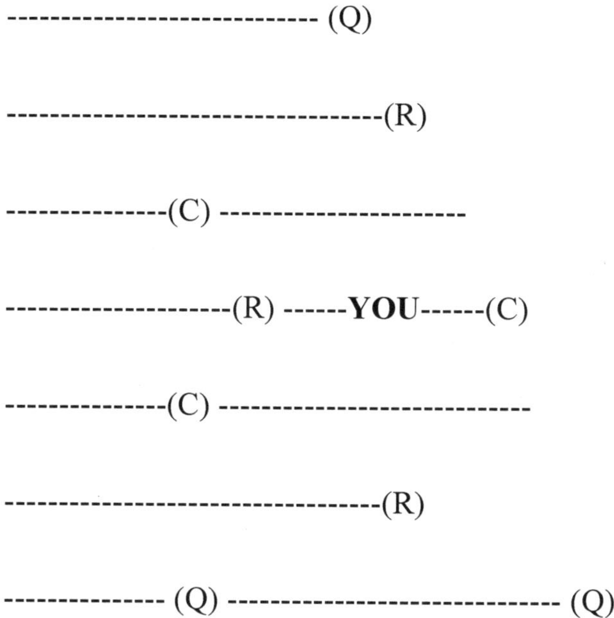

The YOU can be just you or you and a partner. Each group of 3 stones creates a triangle, for 3 triangles total.

Construct this right before you are to try any of the OBE Sex (astral, dream or telepathic) methods. For some people it can be too much energy. Until you can see how it affects you - make sure you set an alarm for 10 min tops so that your energy body can reunite with your physical body and you can assess how strong this energy is. Some people it could make them very aggressive or have them see entities they are not ready to see - for some it could throw their sexual drive off the map.

69 OBE Sex Grid

Supplies:

Mugwort (yes, the herb)

6 Carnelian

9 Crystals (clear or white - not rose or smoky)

69 - yin/yang - male/female is a strong sexual number.

Around your place for OBE sex:

- Sprinkle a circle of Mugwort
- Next evenly space the 6 Carnelian outside of the Mugwort
- Finally evenly space the 9 Crystals outside the Carnelian.

Now YOU are in the middle. Have fun!

OBE and Physical Sex Grid

Need:

8 double terminated Crystals

4 pieces of Copper

1 Moldavite

Powdered Sugar

Cayenne Pepper

On a piece of cardboard or other sturdy, flat material:

- Place 4 Crystals in the shape of a square
- Put the 4 Copper in the open corners
- Take the last 4 Crystals and put them next to the Copper facing into the center of the square.
- Set the Moldavite in the center.
- Sprinkle the grid with Powdered Sugar and Cayenne Pepper.

Move the grid under you bed, preferably in the center if you can reach.

The above grid will certainly improve your sex life. But if you find that you are having a difficult time sleeping, replace the Moldavite with Amethyst or Kunzite, and you'll sleep. When you need the OBE boost put back the Moldavite.

Wearable Telepathic Sex Grid

Now this can be a bit tricky to pull off. But it is seriously doable because I did it!

1. Take 1/8 cup of almond oil and add 9 drops of mugwort oil (or 1/4 tsp. of the herb).
2. Put a tiny quartz crystal into the oil.
3. Put a lid on the oil and set aside, in the dark, for 3 days.
4. Place a dab of infused oil on each temple and right above your genitalia. The two dabs on your temples and the one above your genitalia form an energetic triangle.
5. Wear a moldavite pendant. If you do not have moldavite - get some. If not possible, make it a Faden quartz or regular quartz crystal. Make sure the length of the chain has the pendant lay in between your breasts or chest muscles.

And BOOM. There you go! The stored oil is good for 3 months. Each time you go out and you think you may need a boost, put some on!

OBE Sex Grid & Elixir

Need:

- 3 terminated quartz crystals

- 1 small & 1 medium ceramic or glass bowls
- 1 red jasper
- Spring water
- 1 Faden quartz
- Mugwort - dried herb or essential oil
- Optional: container with lid, plastic wrap

Instructions:

1. Fill the medium bowl 1/2 way with spring water.
2. Place the red jasper & Faden quartz in the small bowl.
3. Sprinkle a couple of pinches of the herb Mugwort or 3 drops of the oil on top the stones.
4. Place the small bowl inside of the medium bowl.
5. *If you want to use the water as an elixir, cover the bowls with plastic wrap.
6. Put the bowl/s in the center of your OBE space. If you can arrange it so that the moon and sun could shine on the bowl/s - double bonus.
7. Arrange the 3 terminated crystals around you/bowl, terminated points facing bowl/you. I like to think of the formation of the crystals as a triangle. Distance between you/bowls and crystals do not matter, as long as they occupy the same space/room.

Important: Doesn't matter where you set this up. Or how big or small it is. What is important is that you and the bowl/s are both in the center.

- You can keep the grid up for as long as you want to. When you are ready to engage in OBE sex, sit or lie down next to/on top of the bowl/s.
- If you want to super charge it & use as an elixir, place the bowl/s in the moonlight/sunlight for 3 days. If the moon and sun can get to where the bowl/s is in the grid, leave it where it is. No need to move it.
- If using as an elixir, do not leave the water in the bowls longer than 3 days. Pour infused water into container and place in fridge.
- You can keep making more infused water using the same stones, crystals, and bowls. Just change out the Mugwort each time.

CHAPTER NINE:
OBE Sex Magic

What Is Magic

The easiest way to tell you what magic is, is to tell you what it isn't: a quick fix. Instant gratification only arrives in the movies or on TV. There is no real Harry Potter or Charmed magic – at least nothing we mere mortals can conjure up.

At its simplest, magic is the ability to manipulate energy, to direct it to where we need a little extra guidance. When a spell is cast, we are giving our energy an added push to help us achieve a dream or goal. Magic is an added boost – a leg up if you will – but be forewarned that it can take up to six months to a year in order to see the fruits of your labor. Sometimes, however, if you're lucky you can start to see results in as little as twenty-four hours.

The energy that surges within each of our bodies is the same energy that soars through the universe and on up into the heavens. It is all around us twenty-four hours a day, seven days a week. Therefore, it is within your reach to take the energy you need to bring about the changes you desire – no special gifts or powers required. Each and every one of us is already blessed with the Divine gifts we require. But to have your magic work, you must firmly and sincerely believe, without a doubt, that you will achieve the results you need. Anything less will result in either complete failure or level of success only achieved by half.

The most important ingredient for a successful magical outcome is thought. Our thoughts are comprised of energy, energy that we normally allow to jump from place to place, person to person throughout the day. Thus, your thoughts affect the people around you as well as impact your life in ways large and small. Since most of the time we do not put forth the effort to control our thoughts, our lives always seem to be awash in confusion.

Magic helps you concentrate your thoughts towards a specific outcome or goal. Once your focus is centered, clear and full of positive passion, determination and resolve, you raise your vibrational rate to match the energy of the Divine. Once your awareness is raised, you can manifest whatever it is that you desire, receiving what your thoughts project. This gives a whole new layer to the phrase, "Be careful what you wish for, as you just might get it."

By tapping into the Divine, where all of our unconscious minds are eternally linked, you are able to influence a person's thought process on an unconscious level, thereby affecting their life on a conscious level. So, magic is nothing more – and nothing less – than having the ability to manipulate the energy around you. We all have the power to make change.

Just think what you can accomplish if you set your mind to it!

Tips for Successful Magic

- Turn off the phone, radio, email, or anything else that will disturb you during the process. However, soothing music may be played as you prepare and perform magic. The key here is that you want no interruptions.

- Keep the tools you use for magic away from other people, as tools absorb the energy of their user.

- Consult a calendar to time your magic with the ebb and flow of the lunar cycle: Waxing and the full moon are best for positive OBE sex and waning is best for pushing someone away or protection in the OBE realm.

- Magic has a very hard time working correctly during a Mercury Retrograde and should be avoided during this time. Mercury figuratively goes backwards (retrograde) four times a year and usually lasts about three weeks. Since Mercury is the planet of communications, you want it to be moving direct for positive results. Don't say I didn't warn you!

- What you send out comes back to you three times over, so if you are using magic to hurt or make someone else feel uncomfortable, you do so at your own risk.

- Keep your magic to yourself. When you tell others of your plans, you invite their energy to mingle in with yours. This can weaken your energy, thereby weakening the energy of your magic.

- Think positively about the changes you desire, but don't dwell on them. By detaching yourself you let the universe help as well. Detaching doesn't decrease the power of the want, but it does give the universe permission to step in and take over.

- Remember that impatience leads to doubt and doubt invites negativity. Neither nature nor the universe can be rushed. Magic works in Divine time, not human time.
- Remember above all that faith in yourself, faith in magic and positive thoughts are all powerful vibratory forces that bring results.

OBE Incenses

OBE Incenses

Incense emits specific vibrations to facilitate transformation. Its energies mix with those of the seeker to speed up the changes needed to reach a desired goal.

Supplies

Mortar and pestle or electric grinder

Non-metal bowl

Glass jar with lid

Charcoal block

Censer

Making Incenses

1. If not purchased pre-powdered, grind each herb into a fine powder using either mortar and pestle or an electric grinder.
2. Add each herb into your bowl.
3. Visualize your need or goal.
4. Once it has been clearly formed in your mind, using your projective hand (right if right-handed, left if left-handed) mix the herbs as the images from your mind transfer down your arm, through your hand and empower the herbs.

5. Store in a tightly capped jar or burn on a block of charcoal. If weather permits, open the window while the incense smolders.

Tips:

- If you are missing an herb, and you have sufficient herbs for the incense, you can substitute the essential oil for the herb.
- When using charcoal blocks, light it from the side. Keep unused blocks in an airtight case.
- Wait until the charcoal block turns white before you add your incense.
- Censers can be anything that is nonflammable and non-metal, from ceramic bowls to sand to everything in-between.
- When burning an incense to GET RID of something: weather permitting, open a window to allow the negative energy to flow out and away from your space.

Incense Blends

Astral Travel

The Best Time

Create this incense when the moon is new, waxing or full.

Herbs

1 tsp. Benzoin

1 tsp. Sandalwood

1 tsp. Mugwort

1 tsp. Dittany of Crete

Lucid Dream Travel

The Best Time

Create this incense when the moon is waxing or full.

Herbs

2 tsp. Mugwort

1 tsp. Jasmine

1 tsp. Spearmint

Increase Vibrational Energy

The Best Time

Create this incense when the moon is waxing or full.

Herbs

1 tsp. Frankincense

1 tsp. Myrrh

1 tsp. Vetiver

1 tsp. Patchouli

1 Bay Leaf

Spiritual Bodyguard

The Best Time

Create this incense when the moon is full.

Herbs

1 tsp. Cinquefoil

1 tsp. Vervain

1 tsp. Peppermint

1 tsp. Dried Garlic

1 Bay Leaf

Remove Astral Residue

The Best Time

Create this incense when the moon is full or waning.

Herbs

2 tsp. Frankincense

2 tsp. Salt

2 tsp. Black Peppercorns

1 tsp. Mugwort

OBE Oils

OBE Oils

Oils can be added to magical tools, placed in a diffuser and applied to personal belongings.

You will need base oil in order to make each different blend.

Base Oils

Almond

Aloe Vera

Apricot Kernel

Coconut

Grapeseed

Hazelnut

Jojoba

Olive

Palm

Rosehip Seed

Safflower

Sunflower

Storage

Store the oils away from all sources of heat, light and moisture. **DO NOT STORE IN THE BATHROOM.** It's best to place your oils in dark-colored, airtight glass bottles, and label each for use.

Stones/Crystals for Oils

If you cannot obtain the stone(s) listed in the recipe, you can substitute a Clear Quartz Crystal.

For extra strength, add a Clear Quartz Crystal with the listed stone. Crystals are natural energizers.

Remember to treat the stones and crystal spirit used in these formulas with respect. Thank these spirits before you add them to the oil for their help in your quest.

Buying Oils

There are many companies that sell oils. Some are genuine essential oils, extracted from the plants for which they are named, while others are blends or bouquets that are actually a mixture of essential oils to arrive at a certain scent. Many places offer either partially or completely synthetic oils, but most are not labeled as such.

For magic it is best to use the genuine article – essential oils. Since they contain the magical essence of the plant, they are the most favorable way to go.

A good way to tell the difference between synthetic and essential oil is price. Essential oils are expensive, but their potency and ultimate success make them well worth the price.

Making the Oils

1. Place your base oil and essentials oils within reach.
2. Begin by visualizing your need or goal.
3. Once it is clearly formed in your mind, add the base oil to the jar.
4. Add the ingredients in one by one, swirling the jar clockwise to mix. Note how each ingredient affects the aroma of the oil.
5. Take your stone/crystal and place it in your projective hand.
6. Visualize your need or goal.
7. Once it has been clearly formed in your mind, pour your need into the stone/crystal.
8. Add the stone/crystal to the oils.
9. Seal the jar.
10. Store for three days (or at least overnight) before your first use.

Oil Blends

Astral Travel

The Best Time

Create this oil when the moon is waxing or full.

Supplies

1/8 cup Base Oil

6 drops Mugwort

6 drops Caraway

6 drops Frankincense

6 drops Petitgrain

1 Bay Leaf - Crushed

(Add 3 drops Vanilla Absolute {the oil, not the vodka} for Astral Sex)

1 Tiny Ametrine, Angelite, Apophyllite, Brazilian Agate, or Opal

1 Sterilized Glass Bottle with Lid

Uses

- Anoint yourself with a few drops on the temples, third-eye (in the center of your forehead), neck at the base of the skull, top of the head, wrists and ankles, prior to travel.

- Anoint candles and burn prior to travel.
- Anoint stones/crystals.
- Place a few drops on a cotton ball or handkerchief and inhale when needed.
- Place a couple of drops in a diffuser.
- Add a few drops to a spray bottle full of spring water and spritz your body.

Telepathic Aid

The Best Time

Create this oil when the moon is full.

Supplies

1/8 cup Base Oil

6 drops Jasmine

3 drops Mugwort

3 drops Rosemary

1/8 tsp. Orris Root

1 Tiny Faden Quartz Crystal, Herkimer Diamond or Tiger's-Eye

1 Sterilized Glass Bottle with Lid

Uses

- Anoint yourself with a few drops on the temples, third-eye (in the center of your forehead), neck at the base of the skull, top of the head, wrists and ankles, prior to trying to make a connection.
- Anoint candles and burn while you try to connect.
- Anoint stones/crystals.
- Place a few drops on a cotton ball or handkerchief and inhale when needed.
- Place a couple of drops in a diffuser.
- Add a few drops to a spray bottle full of spring water and spritz your body.

Dream Protection

The Best Time

Create this oil when the moon is full.

Supplies

1/8 cup Base Oil

6 drops Spearmint

5 drops Vetivert

3 drop Juniper

2 drops Pine

1 Tiny Chalcedony or Turquoise

1 Sterilized Glass Bottle with Lid

Uses

- Anoint yourself with a few drops on the temples, third-eye (in the center of your forehead) neck, wrists and ankles, especially prior to going to sleep.
- Anoint candles and burn prior to sleep.
- Anoint stones/crystals.
- Anoint your pillow.
- Place a few drops on a cotton ball or handkerchief and inhale when needed.
- Add six to ten drops in your bathwater.
- Place a couple of drops in a diffuser.
- Add a few drops to a spray bottle full of spring water and spritz your bed sheets.

Astral Protection

The Best Time

Create this oil when the moon is full.

Supplies

1/8 cup Base Oil

6 drops Geranium

4 drops Black Pepper

3 drops Juniper

2 drops Pine

1/2 tsp. Salt

1 Tiny Chalcedony, Onyx or Opal

1 Sterilized Glass Bottle with Lid

Uses

- Anoint yourself with a few drops on the temples, third-eye (in the center of your forehead), neck at the base of the skull, top of the head, wrists and ankles, prior to travel.
- Anoint candles and burn prior to travel.
- Anoint stones/crystals.
- Place a few drops on a cotton ball or handkerchief and inhale when needed.
- Place a couple of drops in a diffuser.
- Add a few drops to a spray bottle full of spring water and spritz your body.

Erotic Dreams

The Best Time

Create this oil when the moon is new, waxing or full.

Supplies

1/8 cup Base Oil

6 drops Patchouli

3 drops Sandalwood

3 drops Cardamom

1/8 tsp. Sage, powdered or 2 drops Clary Sage

1 Amethyst or Clear Quartz Crystal

1 Sterilized Glass Bottle with Lid

Uses

- Anoint yourself with a few drops on the temples, third-eye (in the center of your forehead) neck, wrists and ankles, especially prior to going to sleep.
- Anoint candles and burn prior to sleep.
- Anoint stones/crystals.
- Anoint your pillow.
- Place a few drops on a cotton ball or handkerchief and inhale when needed.
- Add six to ten drops in your bathwater.

- Place a couple of drops in a diffuser.
- Add a few drops to a spray bottle full of spring water and spritz your bed sheets.

Lucid Dreams

The Best Time

Create this oil when the moon is new, waxing or full.

Supplies

1/8 cup Base Oil

6 drops Mugwort

3 drops Lavender

3 drops Benzoin

1/8 tsp. Sage, powdered or 2 drops Clary Sage

1 Tiny Amethyst or Clear Crystal Quartz

1 Sterilized Glass Bottle with Lid

Uses

- Anoint yourself with a few drops on the temples, third-eye (in the center of your forehead) neck, wrists and ankles, especially prior to going to sleep.
- Anoint candles and burn prior to sleep.

- Anoint stones/crystals.
- Anoint your pillow.
- Place a few drops on a cotton ball or handkerchief and inhale when needed.
- Add six to ten drops in your bathwater.
- Place a couple of drops in a diffuser.
- Add a few drops to a spray bottle full of spring water and spritz your bed sheets.

Dream Recall

The Best Time

Create this oil when the moon is full.

Supplies

1/8 cup Base Oil

9 drops Frankincense

6 drops Clove

3 drops Sandalwood

2 drops Rosemary

1 Tiny Apophyllite, Aventurine or Clear Crystal Quartz

1 Sterilized Glass Bottle with Lid

Uses

- Anoint yourself with a few drops on the temples, third-eye (in the center of your forehead), neck at the base of the skull, top of the head, wrists and ankles, especially prior to going to sleep.
- Anoint candles and burn prior to sleep.
- Anoint stones/crystals.
- Anoint your pillow.
- Anoint Dream Diary.
- Place a few drops on a cotton ball or handkerchief and inhale when needed.
- Add six to ten drops in your bathwater.
- Place a couple of drops in a diffuser.
- Add a few drops to a spray bottle full of spring water and spritz your bed sheets.

OBE Sachets

OBE Sachets

Magical sachets – also known as charms, amulets or talismans – can ward off certain energies or attract a specific energy to you. They can be worn or carried as a personal energy enhancer, or placed in your home to energize your living space.

Material for Sachets

If at all possible, use natural fiber material such as cotton, wool or felt. Same goes for the cord; wool yarn or cotton thread/twine ribbons are ideal materials to use, as synthetic materials seem to interfere with the herbal magic.

The size of the cloth used for a personal sachet should be smaller than one used for the home. Where there's a bigger area to cover then you need more material, i.e. a bigger cloth. I personally like to use cloth pouches – everything fits in nice and neat.

Making Sachets

1. Add each herb into your bowl.
2. Visualize your need or goal.
3. Once it has been clearly formed in your mind, using your projective hand (right if right-handed) mix the herbs as the

images from your mind transfer down your arm, through your hand and empower the herbs.

4. Take your stone/crystal and place it in your projective hand.
5. Visualize your need or goal.
6. Once it has been clearly formed in your mind, pour your need into the stone/crystal.
7. Thank the stone/crystal spirit for its help in your quest.
8. Place the herbs and the stone/crystal in the pouch or tie in cloth.

A Clear Quartz Crystal may be substituted for any stone.

Using Sachets

To activate: Hold the sachet in your hand, squeezing gently to release its fragrance. Carry it with you at all times or place in the appropriate spot.

Three months to the date it was made, bury the herbs and continue to use your sachet to hold your crystal/stone.

Sachet Blends

Astral Travel

The Best Time

Create this sachet when the moon is new, waxing or full.

Supplies Needed

4 Tbsp. Mugwort

3 Tbsp. Sandalwood

2 Tbsp. Cinnamon

2 Tbsp. Dittany of Crete

A Strand of Your Hair

1 Angelite, Apophyllite, Quartz Crystal, or Faden Quartz

1 Non-metal bowl

1 Blue or Silver Pouch or Cloth

1 Thread/Ribbon if Cloth used

Astral Sex

The Best Time

Create this sachet when the moon is full.

Supplies Needed

4 Tbsp. Mugwort

3 Tbsp. Patchouli

2 Tbsp. Sandalwood

2 Tbsp. Damiana

Your Sexual Fluids, Menstrual Blood or Strand of Hair

1 Angelite, Amethyst, Apophyllite, or Moonstone

1 Non-metal bowl

1 Red or Silver Pouch or Cloth

1 Thread/Ribbon if Cloth used

Telepathic Support

The Best Time

Create this sachet when the moon is waxing or full.

Supplies Needed

3 Tbsp. Caraway

3 Tbsp. Ginger

2 Tbsp. Thyme

2 Tbsp. Clover

Two Magnets

1 Amethyst, Faden Quartz Crystal, or Kunzite

1 Non-metal bowl

1 Yellow or Gold Pouch or Cloth

1 Thread/Ribbon if Cloth used

Dream Remembrance

The Best Time

Create this sachet when the moon is full.

Supplies Needed

4 Tbsp. Rosemary

2 Tbsp. Mugwort

2 Tbsp. Juniper

2 Tbsp. Camphor

1 Bay Leaf

A Book Charm and/or a Small Pen

1 Apophyllite, Clear Quartz Crystal, Tiger's-Eye, or Turquoise

1 Non-metal bowl

1 Silver or Purple Pouch or Cloth

1 Thread/Ribbon if Cloth used

Lucid Dream Power

The Best Time

Create this sachet when the moon is full.

Supplies Needed

4 Tbsp. Jasmine

3 Tbsp. Rosemary

3 Tbsp. Lavender

2 Tbsp. Caraway

A Strand of Your Hair

1 Clear Quartz Crystal or Rutilated Quartz Crystal

1 Non-metal bowl

1 Blue or Yellow Pouch or Cloth

1 Thread/Ribbon if Cloth used

Dream Guardian

The Best Time

Create this sachet when the moon is full.

Supplies Needed

3 Tbsp. Agrimony

3 Tbsp. Mugwort

3 Tbsp. Anise Seed

1 Tbsp. Calendula Flowers

1 Tbsp. Dandelion Root

A Strand of Your Hair

1 Black Tourmaline, Cat's-Eye, or Onyx

1 Non-metal bowl

1 Black or Blue Pouch or Cloth

1 Thread/Ribbon if Cloth used

Astral Travel Guardian

The Best Time

Create this sachet when the moon is full.

Supplies Needed

2 Tbsp. Frankincense

2 Tbsp. Kava Kava

2 Tbsp. Mugwort

1 Tbsp. Damiana

1 Bay Leaf

A Strand of Hair

1 Onyx, Tiger's-Eye, or Turquoise

1 Non-metal bowl

1 White or Blue Pouch or Cloth

1 Thread/Ribbon if Cloth used

Metaphysical Aids

Metaphysical OBE Aids

In case you do not want to mix anything together and you want some quick help.

STONES/CRYSTALS TO UTILIZE

Hold one or more of these stones, in your receptive hand (your non-dominant hand) or place them in your environment for an added boost when traveling the OBE!

Amethyst

Apophyllite

Aventurine

Azurite

Beryl

Citrine

Crystal, Faden

Crystal, Clear Crystal, Quartz

Crystal, Rutile

Crystal, Tourmalated

Emerald

Herkimer Diamond

Lapis Lazuli

Linarite

Lepidolite

Kunzite

Moldavite

Moonstone

Opal

Sugilite

Tiger's-Eye

Turquoise

Ulexite

HERBS TO UTILIZE

These herbs can be burned as an incense (burn mixed with Sandalwood or Frankincense), used as tea (although most of these taste really bad), or placed in a sachet/cloth to carry right before or during the time when you want to boost your OBE skills.

Acacia

Althea

Bay

Cinnamon

Citron

Dittany of Crete

Frankincense

Honeysuckle

Mugwort

Peppermint

Poplar

Rose

Rowan

Saffron

Star Anise

Thyme

Uva Ursa

Wormwood

Yarrow

Yerba Santa

OILS TO UTILIZE

These oils can be applied topically (if the oils burn the skin - remove immediately and add a few drops with a base oil such as Sunflower, Olive, Jojoba and then reapply), added to bathwater, placed on a cotton ball or straight from the bottle and inhaled or burned in a diffuser right before or during the time when you want to boost your OBE skills.

Acacia

Anise

Bay

Cardamom

Celery

Cinnamon (will burn if applied directly to skin)

Clary Sage

Ginger

Heliotrope

Iris

Jasmine

Lemongrass

Lilac

Magnolia

Mimosa

Mugwort (will burn if applied directly to skin)

Myrrh

Nutmeg

Patchouli

Rose

Sandalwood

Vanilla

Yarrow

Ylang-Ylang

Appendix and Useful Bits

More About OBE

Join the Out of Body Ecstasy Community on Facebook:

https://www.facebook.com/obesex

To Learn More About Out of Body Ecstasy:

www.OutofBodyEcstasy.com

Useful Links

Magical Supplies

Alchemy Works

http://www.alchemy-works.com

The Eye of the Cat

http://www.eyeofthecat.net/

The Magickal Cat

http://www.themagickalcat.com/

The Realm of White Magic

http://www.magic.com.au/

Essential Oils

Esoteric Oils

http://www.essentialoils.co.za

Flower Essence Services

http://www.fesflowers.com/tfeo1.htm

Stones/Crystals

Best Crystals

http://www.bestcrystals.com/

Metaphysical Realm1

https://www.metaphysicalrealm1.com/

Herbs

Vitacost

http://www.vitacost.com/

Swanson Health Products

http://www.swansonvitamins.com/

Everyday Vitamin

http://www.everydayvitamin.com/

About the Author, Allie Theiss

Allie Theiss helps women take their **passion & desire out of hibernation**. Her special gift is in *igniting*, inspiring, motivating, and *empowering* women who WANT to have it all to stand up and TAKE back their Goddess power.

Allie is a **Holistic Sex Coach, Energy Specialist, and Soul Mate Magnet** as well as a 6th generation intuitive. She's the creator of Out of Body Ecstasy and Red Hot 180.

Previously she ran an erotica audio company for women called Whispers Media where she wrote the sensual audio script, did sex toy reviews, and sex Q & A. At that same time, Allie was also the sexpert for **Showtime's the "L" Word online world in Second Life.**

Allie has her BA & Master's in Psychology and had the privilege of earning her certificate in professional sex coaching with **two world-renowned sexologists: Dr. Patti Britton and Dr. Robert Dunlap.**

To find out more **about Allie, her coaching packages, blog posts, books, and newsletter**, please visit **AllieTheiss.com**

Sex Toys & Passion Zone podcast:

http://www.ThePassionZone.com

Soul Mates & Twin Flame:

http://www.TwinFlameSoulMate.com

Red Hot 180:

http://www.RedHot180.com

Made in the USA
Columbia, SC
03 February 2021